Table of content

Introduction

Chapter one: Biography of the candidates

Chapter two: The economy

Chapter three: Employment and jobs

Chapter four: Terrorism and national security

Chapter five: Education.

Chapter six: Healthcare

Chapter seven: Taxation

Chapter eight: Immigration

Chapter nine: Gun policy.

Chapter ten: Climate change

Chapter eleven: Wall Street and bank regulation and reform

Chapter twelve foreign trades

Introduction.

The book Hillary Clinton versus Donald Trump who suits the white house gives a clear analysis of who the 2016 American presidential candidates are and their ideologies. Who they are in the sense of their personality, their capabilities and background and their ideology in the sense of what the candidates believes in politically economically etc and what they have propose to the if elected. The book is divided into twelve chapters starting with the biography of the candidates down to economic ideologies to immigration policies and other problems of America and how they propose to tackle it if elected.

The book compares the candidates without bias and gives the reader a broad knowledge of the things he/she needs to know before taking decision on whom to vote in the upcoming presidential election.

Chapter one

Biography of the candidates

Biography of Hillary Clinton (Democratic Party nominee)

Hillary Diane Clinton was born Hillary Diane Rodham on October 26, 1947, in Chicago, Illinois. She was raised in Park Ridge, Illinois, a picturesque suburb located 15 miles northwest of downtown Chicago.

Hillary Rodham was the eldest daughter of Hugh Rodham, a prosperous fabric store owner, and Dorothy Emma Howell Rodham; she has two younger brothers, Hugh Jr. (born 1950) and Anthony (born 1954).

As a young woman, Hillary was active in young Republican groups and campaigned for Republican presidential nominee Barry Goldwater in 1964. She was inspired to work in some form of public service after hearing a speech in Chicago by the Reverend Martin Luther King Jr., and became a Democrat in 1968.

Education and Early Career

Rodham attended Wellesley College, where she was active in student politics and elected senior class president before graduating in 1969. She then attended Yale Law School, where she met Bill Clinton. Graduating with honors in 1973, she went on to enroll at Yale Child Study Center, where she took courses on children and medicine and completed one post-graduate year of study.

Hillary worked at various jobs during her summers as a college student. In 1971, she first came to Washington, D.C. to work on U.S. Senator Walter Mondale's sub-committee on migrant workers. In the summer of 1972, she worked in the western states for the campaign of Democratic presidential nominee George McGovern.

In the spring of 1974, Rodham became a member of the presidential impeachment inquiry staff, advising the Judiciary Committee of the House of Representatives during the Watergate Scandal.

(Chief Counsel Jerry Zeifman would later contend that he fired Clinton from the committee for what he deemed as unethical professional behavior connected to Nixon's due process. These allegations have been contradicted by other media sources that deny Zeifman's authority over the young attorney at this time, with no comment from Clinton herself.)

After President Richard M. Nixon resigned in August, she became a faculty member of the University of Arkansas Law School in Fayetteville, where her Yale Law School classmate and boyfriend Bill Clinton was teaching as well.

Marriage to Bill Clinton

Hillary Rodham married Bill Clinton on October 11, 1975, at their home in Fayetteville. Before he proposed marriage, Clinton had secretly purchased a small house that she had remarked that she liked. When he proposed marriage to her and she accepted, he revealed that they owned the house. Their daughter, Chelsea Victoria, was born on February 27, 1980.

In 1976, Hillary worked on Jimmy Carter's successful campaign for president while husband Bill was elected attorney general.

Bill Clinton was elected governor in 1978 at age 32, lost reelection in 1980, but came back to win in 1982, 1984, 1986 (when the term of office was expanded from two to four years) and 1990.

Hillary joined the Rose Law Firm in Little Rock and, in 1977, was appointed to part-time chairman of the Legal Services Corporation by President Carter. As first lady of the state for a dozen years (1979-1981, 1983-1992), she chaired the Arkansas Educational Standards Committee, co-founded the Arkansas Advocates for Children and Families, and served on the boards of the Arkansas Children's Hospital, Arkansas Legal Services and the Children's Defense Fund. She also served on the boards of TCBY and Wal-Mart.

In 1988 and 1991, The National Law Journal named her one of the 100 most powerful lawyers in America.

First Lady

During Bill Clinton's 1992 presidential campaign, Hillary emerged as a dynamic and valued partner of her husband, and as president he named her to head the Task Force on National Health Reform (1993). The controversial commission produced a complicated plan which never came to the floor of either house. It was abandoned in September 1994.

During this period, she and her husband invested in the Whitewater real estate project. The project's bank, Morgan Guaranty Savings and Loan, failed, costing the federal government $73 million. Whitewater later became the subject of congressional hearings and an independent counsel investigation.

In 1998, the White House was engulfed in the Monica Lewinsky sex scandal. Though she publicly supported her husband, Mrs. Clinton reportedly considered leaving her marriage. He was impeached, but the U.S. Senate failed to convict and he remained in office.

Senate Win and Presidential Run

With her husband limited to two terms in the White House, Mrs. Clinton decided she would seek the U.S. Senate seat from New York held by Daniel Patrick Moynihan. He was retiring after four terms. Despite early problems and charges of carpetbagging, Clinton beat popular Republican Rick Lazio by a surprisingly wide margin: 55 percent to 43 percent. Clinton became the first wife of a president to seek and win public office and the first woman to be elected to the U.S. Senate from New York. She easily won reelection in November 2006.

In early 2007, Clinton announced her plans to strive for another first—to be the first female president. During the 2008 Democratic primaries, Senator Clinton conceded the nomination when it became apparent that nominee Barack Obama held a majority of the delegate vote. When Clinton suspended her campaign, she made a speech to her supporters. "Although we were not able to shatter that highest and hardest glass ceiling this time, thanks to you it has 18 million cracks in it," she said, "and the light is shining through like never before, filling us all with the hope and the sure knowledge that the path will be a little easier next time, and we are going to keep working to make it so, today keep with me and stand for me, we still have so much to do together, we made history, and lets make some more."

U.S. Secretary of State

Shortly after winning the U.S. presidential election, Obama nominated Hillary Clinton as secretary of state. She accepted the nomination and was officially approved as the 67th U.S. secretary of state by the Senate on January 21, 2009.

During her term, Clinton used her position to make women's rights and human rights a central talking point of U.S. initiatives. She became one of the most traveled secretaries of state in American history, and promoted the use of social media to convey the country's positions. She also led U.S. diplomatic efforts in connection to the Arab Spring and military intervention in Libya.

The State Department, under Clinton's leadership, came under investigation after a deadly attack on a U.S. diplomatic post in Benghazi, Libya, killed U.S. ambassador Christopher Stevens and three others on September 11, 2012. An independent panel issued a report about the Benghazi attack, which found "systematic failures and leadership and management deficiencies" at the State Department.

Health Issues

Clinton, who said she took responsibility for security at the outpost in Benghazi, was scheduled to testify about the attack before Congress in December 2012. She canceled her scheduled testimony, however, citing a stomach virus and, later, a concussion that she suffered after fainting (the cause of which was later reported as dehydration). Some members of Congress questioned the timing of Clinton's illnesses, including Representative Allen West, who stated that he believed the secretary of state was suffering from "a case of Benghazi flu" on the day she was scheduled to testify.

On December 30, 2012, Clinton was hospitalized with a blod clot related to the concussion that she had suffered earlier in the month. She was released from a New York hospital on January 2, 2013, after receiving treatment, and soon recovered and returned to work.

Benghazi Testimony and Resignation

Clinton's testimony on the Benghazi attack came on January 23, 2013. Speaking to members of the House Foreign Relations Committee, she defended her actions while taking full responsibility for the incident, which killed four American citizens. "As I have said many times since September 11, I take responsibility, and nobody is more committed to getting this right," she told the House. She added, "I am determined to leave the State Department and our country safer, stronger and more secure."

Since taking office in 2009, Clinton repeatedly stated over the years that she was only interested in serving one term as secretary of state. She officially stepped down from her post on February 1, 2013.

In May 2014, the House Select Committee on Benghazi, chaired by Representative Trey Gowdy from South Carolina, was created to investigate the Benghazi attack. Clinton testified in front of the committee on October 22, 2015 in a nearly 11-hour hearing. The House Select Committee on

Benghazi issued its final report on June 28, 2016. The just over 800-page report found no new evidence of wrongdoing on Clinton's part, but was critical of "government agencies like the Defense Department, the Central Intelligence Agency and the State Department — and the officials who led them — for failing to grasp the acute security risks in the Libyan city, and especially for maintaining outposts in Benghazi that they could not protect," according to The New York Times.

The Democrats on the committee issued their own 339-page minority report that criticized Republicans for "one of the longest and most partisan congressional investigations in history" that took two years to complete and cost "$7 million in taxpayer funds."

"We have been hampered in our work by the ongoing Republican obsession with conspiracy theories that have no basis in reality," the minority report stated. "Rather than reject these conspiracy theories in the absence of evidence — or in the face of hard facts — Select Committee Republicans embraced them and turned them into a political crusade."

Mother-in-Law and Grandmother

In 2010 Clinton's daughter Chelsea married former Goldman Sachs investment banker and current hedge fund manager Marc Mezvinksy.

On September 26, 2014, Clinton became a first-time grandmother when daughter Chelsea gave birth to Charlotte Clinton Mezvinsky. Chelsea gave birth to her second child Aidan Clinton Mezvinsky on June 18, 2016.

Bid for 2016 Presidency

In June 2014, Clinton released Hard Choices, a memoir published by Simon & Schuster, which rose to number one on the New York Times Best Seller list. The following year in early March 2015, Clinton faced controversy and criticism when it was revealed that she had used her personal email address to handle official governmental business during her time as secretary of state. In a news conference held at the United Nations, speaking initially on gender equality and the political situation in Iran, Clinton stated that she had utilized her personal email for convenience as allowed by state department protocol. She later turned over all governmental correspondence to the Obama administration while deleting messages that could be construed as personal. After much speculation and assumptions over whether Clinton would run for the U.S. presidency, her plans were made official in the spring of 2015. On April 12, Clinton's campaign chairperson John D. Podesta announced via email that the former secretary of state was entering the race to secure the Democratic presidential nomination for the 2016 elections. This was immediately followed by an online campaign clip, with Clinton herself announcing that she's running for president at the end of the video.

Campaign Issues

On her campaign site, Clinton discusses a wide variety of issues she believes in, among them: lowering student debt, criminal justice reform, campaign finance reform, improving the healthcare coverage and costs of the Affordable Care Act (a.k.a. Obamacare), and women's rights.

However, she is also known for changing her stances on various hot button issues such as gay marriage (she now supports it) and trade deals (e.g. she is now against the Trans Pacific Partnership). In regard to the environment, Clinton has a plan to combat climate change but has been questioned by environmental activists for supporting fracking. She is also in support of the death penalty but claims it should be implemented in exceptional cases.On June 6, 2016 Clinton was hailed as the presumptive presidential nominee for the Democratic Party and the first woman in the United States' 240-year history "to top the presidential ticket of a major U.S. political party," according to the Associated Press. The assessment was based on Clinton winning the support of a combination of pledged delegates and superdelegates needed to win the nomination.

The biography of Donald Trump. (Republican party nominee)

Donald John Trump (born June 14, 1946) is an American businessman, television personality, author, and the Republican Party nominee for President of the United States in the 2016 election. He is chairman of The Trump Organization, which is the principal holding company for his real estate ventures and other business interests.

Born and raised in New York City, Trump received a bachelor's degree in economics from the Wharton School of the University of Pennsylvania in 1968. While attending college, Trump worked in his father Fred Trump's real estate and construction firm. He assumed control of the business in 1973, and later renamed it The Trump Organization. During his career, Trump has built skyscrapers, hotels, casinos, golf courses, and numerous other developments, many of which bear his name, including Trump Place in Manhattan. He briefly sought the Reform Party's nomination in the 2000 presidential election but withdrew prior to any primary contests. Listed by Forbes among the wealthiest 400 of The World's Billionaires, Trump and his businesses, as well as his personal life, have for decades received prominent media exposure. He hosted The Apprentice, a popular reality television show on NBC, from 2004 to 2015.

In June 2015, Trump announced his candidacy for president as a Republican and quickly emerged as the front-runner for his party's nomination. His platform includes opposition to trade agreements that he regards as unfair, such as NAFTA and TPP, renegotiation of NAFTA and U.S.–China trade deals, immigration enforcement including the building of a wall along the U.S.–Mexico border, reform of veterans' care, replacement of the Affordable Care Act, and tax cuts. He has suggested a temporary suspension of immigration to the United States from nations having a "proven history" of terrorism against the U.S. until more precise vetting techniques can be put in place to screen out potential terrorists; he also believes that the quick defeat of ISIS is mandatory.

Trump's presidential campaign has received extensive media coverage and international attention. His statements in interviews and at campaign rallies have often been controversial, with the rallies sometimes accompanied by protests or riots. Following Trump's victory in the Indiana primary in May 2016, his remaining Republican rivals suspended their campaigns, and in July he was formally nominated for president at the 2016 Republican National Convention.

Chapter two

The economy

Unemployment continues to fall, inflation is in check, interest rates remain near historical lows, the governments of major U.S. partners have no intention to engage in trade wars, and the price of oil and energy continues to fall. There are no major storms in the forecast for the U.S. economy. Nevertheless, very few economists, if any, are forecasting a growth rate of more than 3% for next year. What is holding back the U.S. economy?

Three factors conspire against growth:

 The uncertainties about which road will the U.S. economy will take after the next presidential election;

 The continued high cost of the regulatory state and all its effects, from corruption to arbitrariness; and

The lacklustre performance of most major western economies. Neither the Trans-Pacific Partnership (TPP) nor the Transatlantic Trade and Investment Partnership (TTIP) is perfect. But being perfect and being necessary are two different things. Europe, especially now, needs all the economic growth it can muster. And without the TPP, the rules of trade in Asia will be written without the input of the U.S. Both are critical in their own way. With government debt passing $18 trillion, Obama keeps beating his record of increasing federal borrowing more than any other president in U.S. history. During his tenure, government debt increased by $8 trillion, and as interest rates will continue to be extremely low, the costs will not be felt this year.

Many American voters knew that the situation right now is not good and they want a change. They want Tax Relief to Grow the Economy and Create Jobs, American Competitiveness in a Global Economy and many more. Here are the candidates approach to tackling numerous economic challenges.

Summary of Hillary Clinton proposal on the economy.

Clinton has literally decades of experience in the domestic and international policy trenches. Befitting this background, she has offered a wide range of detailed proposals on everything from renewable energy goals to sick-leave guarantees. Clinton's presidential policy apparatus began with a small group of formal and informal advisers conducting what amounted to a research project on what is wrong with the American economy — and how to fix it. They interviewed about 200 experts.

What she has released so far is the distilled product of that effort. Her plan includes spending more than $1 trillion to rebuild U.S. infrastructure, allow students to attend college without incurring debt and help working families afford day care for their children and take paid leave to raise them. She thinks such spending would create jobs and accelerate economic growth, help low- and middle-income students gain skills that are increasingly necessary for high-wage work, and reverse a recent trend of women leaving the U.S. workforce. She would raise taxes on the highest earners and impose a new minimum effective tax rate for them, to pay for those programs and to curb inequality. She would add to the Obama administration's wave of new regulations on Wall Street. And she would change the tax code to discourage companies from moving operations overseas, while encouraging them to share profits with workers and invest more in long-term opportunities.

"We skewed the tax code toward the wealthy," Clinton said. "We continued to undermine workers' rights. We have blocked investments in our shared future. And I don't think it's just greed, as serious as that is. It seems we've lost a sense of shared responsibility and forgotten we're all in this together."

Trade isn't the only issue where she's rejected the most liberal wing of her party. She did not endorse a $15-an-hour federal minimum wage -- even though the policy polls well, it was included in the party's platform and it would lift the wages of many working class Americans. Instead, she backs a $12-an-hour federal minimum and the ability for states to set higher ones if they choose. Aides say that is because she thinks that $15 an hour may be too high for states with lower average incomes and costs of living, such as her former home of Arkansas. Clinton's economic plan has drawn praise from a wide range of liberal and center-left policy experts, even when those experts have disagreements about what to do to address middle-class challenges.

She has blended slogans and policy proposals from several top liberal policy thinkers. For example, she talks about the rules of the economy being "rigged" against workers and toward the wealthy and powerful, Coming just eight years after unemployment spiked to 17% in the wake of the 2008 financial crisis, Clinton clearly wants to run on a platform of tougher Wall Street enforcement. And for good reason. Some 67% of the U.S. populace wants a president who favours stricter regulation of financial institutions, according to a Washington Post-ABC News poll conducted in October. Even Republicans to the tune of 58% said they want a candidate willing to toughen Wall Street oversight. Clinton has steadfastly insisted that being paid hundreds of thousands of dollars to speak to financial firms doesn't preclude her from supporting Dodd-Frank or the Consumer Protection Act, the cornerstone of Obama's financial reforms. Clinton said she would seek to re-insert regulations that Republicans took out of the bill in exchange for passage.

First and foremost was a bank tax to help pay to implement the law. Second was the so-called Volcker Rule, aimed at discouraging banks from making risky investments. Clinton has also proposed levying a "graduated risk fee every year on the liabilities of banks with more than $50 billion in assets, and other financial institutions that are designed by regulators for enhanced oversight." Those fees, Clinton says, would be scaled "higher for firms with greater amounts of debt and riskier, short-term forms of debt." Clinton likens it to a deterrent, a rainy day fund. though, Clinton doesn't support restoring Glass-Steagall, which was passed in 1936 in the throes of the Depression to separate commercial banking from investment banking. She insists that even if Glass-Steagall hadn't been repealed, Lehman Brothers, AIG and Bear Stearns, among others, wouldn't have been prevented from making risky bets.

Rather than focusing on Glass-Steagall, Clinton counters that a different kind of regulatory framework is needed to monitor hedge funds and other non-bank institutions, adding that Dodd-Frank could be used to break up banks, if that's what was required. Clinton has been emphasizing in campaign speeches that as president she would seek to close the so-called "carried interest loophole." In effect, the provision allows money managers and hedge fund operators to treat fees on their clients' investments as capital gains, which are taxed at a maximum rate of 23.8% rather than the 39.6% rate applied to ordinary income.

Closing the loophole, and raising taxes on short-term capital gains, are being pitched as concrete steps aimed addressing income inequality, an issue resonating with both Democrats and Republicans.

The carried interest loophole allows "individuals making more than $450 million a year on average are taxed at a lower rate than teachers making around $50,000 on average,

Clinton proposes a fairly cautious agenda -- one that offers a measure of change, but without blowing up the existing system and without bucking long-standing practices such as staying within budget constraints.

Summary of Donald Trump proposal on the economy.

Trump wants to be the "jobs president." In his speech declaring his candidacy for president, he proclaimed, "I will be the greatest jobs president that God ever created."

Trump's big claim is that he will bring back American jobs -- "from China, from Mexico, from Japan, from so many places."

If you listen closely, Trump has proposed doing this two ways: slapping tariffs on foreign goods and negotiating better trade deals. In his campaign announcement speech, he threatened a

35% tax on Ford (F) vehicles made in Mexico that are brought back to the U.S. to be sold, and in 2011, he has made headlines for suggesting a 25% tariff on goods coming from China to the U.S. He says he is against the Obama administration's current Trans-Pacific Partnership -- known as TPP -- but he also espouses, "I am a free trader." In his mind, the problem is that China has better negotiators than the U.S. (even though China is not a part of TPP). Trump says he believes passionately in free trade, but only when the rules are fair and currency is properly valued. He cites a study by the Peterson Institute for International Economics that finds that even a 20 percent revaulation of Chinese currency would create 300,000 to 700,000 American jobs. Trump said "I'm going to be bringing back jobs from China, from Japan, from India, from Brazil. This is going on at a level that you have never seen before. We now have corporate inversions, where companies are moving out of the United States. And they will be moving out in big numbers if we don't do something quickly. And my plan stops all of that. I want to bring back trillions of dollars that is stuck in other countries that we won't let back in because we don't have intelligent people running our country.

In Time to Get Tough, Trump advocated passage of the "No Oil Producing and Exporting Cartels Act (NOPEC—S.394) which would amend the Sherman Antitrust Act to allow the U.S. government to sue OPEC for violating antitrust laws.

Trump notes the bill passed the Senate Judiciary Committee four times with bipartisan backing, "and in May 2008, the NOPEC bill passed the House" before "President George W.

Bush got spooked and threatened to veto the bill" over fears of "retaliatory action" with wars raging in Iraq and Afghanistan.

Passing NOPEC, wrote Trump, would have allowed the U.S. to bust up the OPEC cartel.

"Imagine how much money the average American would save if we busted the OPEC cartel. Imagine how much stronger economic shape we would be in if we made the Iraqi government agree to a cost-sharing plan that paid us back the $1.5 trillion we've dropped on liberating Iraq."

Trump added, "Just those two acts of leadership alone would represent a huge leap forward for our country.

Chapter three

Employment and jobs

U.S. unemployment fell to 4.7%, the lowest rate since 2007. But job creation was very weak.

The U.S. economy only added 38,000 jobs in May, according to the Labor Department. It was the worst monthly job gain since 2010.

It's also well below April's meager job gains of 123,000. Job creation in the last two months has been markedly below the average of 200,000 jobs created per month over the past couple years.

The drop in unemployment came as more disheartened Americans stopped looking for jobs and dropped out of the labor force in May.

'It's a pretty gloomy report, hard to find a silver lining in this one," says Curt Long, chief economist at the National Association of Federal Credit Unions. the U.S. economy is considered to be at or near "full employment" and it's expected that hiring will slow down to a certain degree. In recent months, more Americans had been coming back into the job market. Now the trend appears to be hitting a plateau.

The number of Americans working part-time jobs but want full-time jobs shot up to 6.4 million from about 6 million. These so-called "involuntary" part-time workers have remained a major concern in the job market. Before the recession there were only about 4.2 million such part-timers.

The employment-population ratio has not always been looked at for labor statistics and where specific areas are economically, but after the recent recession it has been given more attention worldwide, especially by economists. The National Bureau Of Economic Research (NBER) states that the recession that began in 2007 ended in June 2009.[5] During 2009 and 2010, however, many areas were still struggling economically, which lies the reason the employment-population ratio still has the eyes of Americans and people around the world.

Summary of Hillary Clinton proposal on jobs and employment

Hillary promised that as president she will Invest in good-paying jobs. In her first 100 days as president, Hillary will work with both parties to make bold investments in infrastructure, manufacturing, research and technology, clean energy, and small businesses. This will create millions of good-paying jobs, including for labor and other hard-working Americans across the country. As an original co-sponsor of the Employee Free Choice Act. Hillary will fight to strengthen the labor movement and to protect worker bargaining power. She will continue to stand up against attacks on collective bargaining and work to strengthen workers' voices.

Hillary will strengthen American trade enforcement so we stand up to foreign countries that aren't playing by the rules— like China is doing right now with steel, and fight for American workers. She will say no to trade deals, like the Trans-Pacific Partnership, that do not meet her high standard of raising wages, creating good-paying jobs, and enhancing our national security.

Raise the minimum wage and strengthen overtime rules. Hillary will work to raise the federal minimum wage to $12, and support state and local efforts to go even higher— including the "Fight for $15." She also supports the Obama administration's expansion of overtime rules to millions more workers. Hillary will reward companies that share profits and invest in their workers. She will crack down on companies that move profits overseas to avoid paying U.S. taxes and she will make companies that export jobs give back the tax breaks they've received in America. She has promised to fight for equal pay for women and guarantee paid leave, two changes that are long overdue. And she will provide relief from the rising costs of necessities like child care and housing. She has promised to Hillary will fight for equal pay for women and guarantee paid leave, two changes that are long overdue. And she will provide relief from the rising costs of necessities like child care and housing. She will Pursue smarter, fairer, tougher trade policies that put U.S. job creation first and get tough on nations like China that seek to prosper at the expense of our workers. This includes opposing trade deals like the Trans-Pacific Partnership that do not meet a high bar of creating good-paying jobs and raising pay.

She said that The measure of our success will be how much incomes rise for hardworking families. How many children are lifted out of poverty. How many Americans can find good jobs that support a middle-class life—and not only that, jobs that provide a sense of dignity and pride. That's what it means to have an economy that works for everyone, not just those at the top. That's the mission, and I'm asking all of you to join me in it.

Summary of Donald Trump proposal on employment and jobs

Trump says "I want to create jobs so that you don't have to worry about the minimum wage. They'll do a great job that they're making much more than the minimum wage. But I think having a low minimum wage is not a bad thing for this country."

Trump believes in eliminating a federal minimum wage. He said, "I don't know how people make it on $7.25 an hour. Now, with that being said, I would like to see an increase of some magnitude. But I'd rather leave it to the states. Let the states decide. Because don't forget, the states have to compete with each other."

At the fourth Republican primary debate on November 2015, Donald Trump said he opposed raising the minimum wage. He said, "People have to go out, they have to work really hard and have to get into that upper stratum. But we can not do this [raise minimum wage] if we are going to compete with the rest of the world. We just can't do it."

During the announcement of his presidential bid on June 16, 2015, Trump claimed, "I will be the greatest jobs president that God ever created. I'll bring back our jobs from China, from Japan from Mexico from so many places. I'll bring back our jobs and I'll bring back our money."

In 2011, while appearing on FOX's "The O'Reilly Factor," Trump said Scott Walker's approach to unions in Wisconsin was appropriate for that state. Trump explained, "I think that he is maybe right for his state. I think it doesn't necessarily apply to all states. You know, I have had great relationship over the years with unions. We've had collective bargaining. I have become very wealthy. I have dealt with unions because, as you know, New York is largely unions. You are dealing with them. I have great friends that are in unions and heads of unions. So I haven't had the same difficulty and problem. But I think you have to do what's right for your area."

Trump believes that trade reform, and the negotiation of great trade deals, is the quickest way to bring our jobs back.

To understand why trade reform creates jobs, we need to understand how all nations grow and prosper.

Massive trade deficits subtract directly from our Gross Domestic Product.

From 1947 to 2001 - a span of over five decades - our inflation-adjusted gross domestic product grew at a rate of 3.5%.

However, since 2002 - the year after we fully opened our markets to Chinese imports - that GDP growth rate has been cut almost in half.

What does this mean for Americans? For every one percent of GDP growth we fail to generate in any given year, we also fail to create over one million jobs.

America's "job creation deficit" due to slower growth since 2002 is well over 20 million jobs - and that's just about the number of jobs our country needs right now to put America back to work at decent wages.

He sees The Transpacific-Partnership as the greatest danger yet.

The TPP would be the death blow for American manufacturing.

It would give up all of our economic leverage to an international commission that would put the interests of foreign countries above our own.

It would further open our markets to aggressive currency cheaters. It would make it easier for our trading competitors to ship cheap subsidized goods into U.S. markets - while allowing foreign countries to continue putting barriers in front of our exports.

The TPP would lower tariffs on foreign cars, while leaving in place the foreign practices that keep American cars from being sold overseas. The TPP even created a backdoor for China to supply car parts for automobiles made in Mexico.

The agreement would also force American workers to compete directly against workers from Vietnam, one of the lowest wage countries on Earth.

Not only will the TPP undermine our economy, but it will undermine our independence.

The TPP creates a new international commission that makes decisions the American people can't veto.

These commissions are great Hillary Clinton's Wall Street funders who can spend vast amounts of money to influence the outcomes.

It should be no surprise then that Hillary Clinton, according to Bloomberg, took a "leading part in drafting the Trans-Pacific Partnership".

She praised or pushed the TPP on 45 separate occasions, and even called it the "gold standard".

Hillary Clinton was totally for the TPP just a short while ago, but when she saw my stance, which is totally against, she was shamed into saying she would be against it too – but have no doubt, she will immediately approve it if it is put before her, guaranteed.

She will do this just as she has betrayed American workers for Wall Street throughout her career.

Here's how it would go: she would make a small token change, declare the pact fixed, and ram it through.

That's why Hillary is now only saying she has problems with the TPP "in its current form," – ensuring that she can rush to embrace it again at her earliest opportunity.

If the media doesn't believe me, I have a challenge for you. Ask Hillary Clinton if she is willing to withdraw from the TPP her first day in office and unconditionally rule out its passage in any form.

There is no way to "fix" the TPP. We need bilateral trade deals. We do not need to enter into another massive international agreement that ties us up and binds us down.

Here are 7 steps he promised to pursue right away to bring back our jobs.

One: I am going to withdraw the United States from the Trans-Pacific Partnership, which has not yet been ratified.

Two: I'm going to appoint the toughest and smartest trade negotiators to fight on behalf of American workers.

Three: I'm going to direct the Secretary of Commerce to identify every violation of trade agreements a foreign country is currently using to harm our workers. I will then direct all appropriate agencies to use every tool under American and international law to end these abuses.

Four: I'm going tell our NAFTA partners that I intend to immediately renegotiate the terms of that agreement to get a better deal for our workers. And I don't mean just a little bit better, I mean a lot better. If they do not agree to a renegotiation, then I will submit notice under Article 2205 of the NAFTA agreement that America intends to withdraw from the deal.

Five: I am going to instruct my Treasury Secretary to label China a currency manipulator. Any country that devalues their currency in order to take advantage of the United States will be met with sharply

Six: I am going to instruct the U.S. Trade Representative to bring trade cases against China, both in this country and at the WTO. China's unfair subsidy behavior is prohibited by the terms of its entrance to the WTO, and I intend to enforce those rules.

Seven: If China does not stop its illegal activities, including its theft of American trade secrets, I will use every lawful presidential power to remedy trade disputes, including the application of tariffs consistent with Section 201 and 301 of the Trade Act of 1974 and Section 232 of the Trade Expansion Act of 1962.

Chapter four

Terrorism and national security

The President's highest priority is to keep the American people safe. He is committed to ensuring the United States is true to our values and ideals while also protecting the American people. The President is committed to securing the homeland against 21st century threats by preventing terrorist attacks and other threats against our homeland, preparing and planning for emergencies, and investing in strong response and recovery capabilities. We will help ensure that the Federal Government works with states and local governments, and the private sector as close partners in a national approach to prevention, mitigation, and response.

There is need to enhance the ability of our partners to improve their own security and work with us to defeat terrorism worldwide. Attacks using improvised nuclear devices or biological weapons, as well as outbreaks of a pandemic disease, pose a serious and increasing national security risk, We need to focus on reducing the risk of these high-consequence, nontraditional threats: Gathering, analyzing, and effectively sharing intelligence is vital to the security of the United States. In order to prevent threats, including those from terrorism, we need to strengthen intelligence collection to identify and interdict those who intend to do us harm. The information we collect must be analyzed as well as shared, and we must invest in our analytic capabilities and our capacity to share intelligence across all levels of government. As we grow our intelligence capabilities, the President is also committed to strengthening efforts to protect the privacy and civil rights of all Americans.

Here are the candidates proposed strategies to enhancing national security and managing terrorism.

Summary of Hillary Clinton proposal on national security and terrorism

Hillary Clintons' has a wholistic approach to handling terrorism and enhancing national security. In her discussion at concil of foreign relation in November 2015 she said "we've seen deadly terrorist attacks in Nigeria, Lebanon, Iraq, and Turkey, and a Russian civilian airline destroyed over the Sinai. At the heat of today's new landscape of terror is ISIS. They persecute religious and ethnic minorities, kidnap and behead civilians, murder children. They systematically enslave, torture, and rape women and girls. ISIS operates across three mutually reinforcing dimensions—a physical enclave in Iraq and Syria, an international terrorist network that includes affiliates across the region and beyond, and an ideological movement of radical jihadism. We have to target and defeat all three.

And time is of the essence. ISIS is demonstrating new ambition, reach, and capabilities. We have to break the group's momentum, and then its back. Our goal is not to deter or contain ISIS but to defeat and destroy ISIS. But we have learned that we can score victories over terrorist leaders and networks only to face metastasizing threats down the road. So we also have to play and win the long game. We should pursue a comprehensive counterterrorism strategy, one that embeds our mission against ISIS within a broader struggle against radical jihadism that is bigger than any one group, whether it's al-Qaida or ISIS or some other network.

An immediate war against an urgent enemy and a generational struggle against an ideology with deep roots will not be easily torn out. It will require sustained commitment in every pillar of American power. This is a worldwide fight, and America must lead it.

Our strategy should have three main elements: one, defeat ISIS in Syria, Iraq, and across the Middle East; two, disrupt and dismantle the growing terrorist infrastructure that facilities the flow of fighters, financing arms, and propaganda around the world; three, harden our defenses and those of our allies against external and homegrown threats.

Let me start with the campaign to defeat ISIS across the region. The United States and our international coalition has been conducting this fight for more than a year. It's time to begin a new phase and intensify and broaden our efforts to smash the would-be caliphate and deny ISIS control of territory in Iraq and Syria.

That starts with a more effective coalition air campaign, with more allies' planes, more strikes, and a broader target set. A key obstacle standing in the way is a shortage of good intelligence about ISIS and its operations. So we need an immediate intelligence surge in the region, including technical assets, Arabic speakers with deep expertise in the Middle East, an even closer partnership with regional intelligence services.

Our goal should be to achieve the kind of penetration we accomplished with al-Qaida in the past. This would help us identify and eliminate ISIS' command and control and its economic lifelines. A more effective coalition air campaign is necessary but not sufficient. And we should be honest about the fact that to be successful, air strikes will have to be combined with ground forces actually taking back more territory from ISIS.

Like President Obama, I do not believe that we should again have 100,000 American troops in combat in the Middle East. That is just not the smart move to make here. If we've learned anything from 15 years of war in Iraq and Afghanistan, it's that local people and nations have to secure their own communities. We can help them, and we should, but we cannot substitute for them. But we can and should support local and regional ground forces in carrying out this mission.

Now, the obstacles to achieving this are significant. On the Iraqi side of the border, Kurdish forces have fought bravely to defend their own lands and to retake towns from ISIS, but the Iraqi National Army has struggled and it's going to take more work to get it up to fighting shape. As part of that process we may have to give our own troops advising and training the Iraqis greater freedom of movement and flexibility, including embedding in local units and helping target airstrikes.

Ultimately, however, the ground campaign in Iraq will only succeed if more Iraqi Sunnis join the fight. But that won't happen so long as they do not feel they have a stake in their country or confidence in their own security and capacity to confront ISIS.

Now, we've been in a similar place before in Iraq. In the first "Sunni awakening" in 2007 we were able to provide sufficient support and assurances to the Sunni tribes to persuade them to join us in rooting out al-Qaida. Unfortunately, under Prime Minister Maliki's rule, those tribes were betrayed and forgotten.

So the task of bringing Sunnis off the sidelines into this new fight will be considerably more difficult. But nonetheless, we need to lay the foundation for a second "Sunni awakening." We need to put sustained pressure on the government in Baghdad to gets its political house in order, move forward with national reconciliation, and finally, stand up a national guard. Baghdad needs to accept, even embrace, arming Sunni and Kurdish forces in the war against ISIS. But if Baghdad won't do that, the coalition should do so directly.

On the Syrian side, the big obstacle to getting more ground forces to engage ISIS beyond the Syrian Kurds, who are already deep in the fight is that the viable Sunni opposition groups remain understandably preoccupied with fighting Assad, who, let us remember, has killed many more Syrians than the terrorists have. But they are increasingly under threat from ISIS as well, so we need to move simultaneously toward a political solution to the civil war that paves the way for a new government with new leadership, and to encourage more Syrians to take on ISIS as well.

To support them, we should immediately deploy the special operations force President Obama has already authorized, and be prepared to deploy more as more Syrians get into the fight. And we should retool and ramp up our efforts to support and equip viable Syrian opposition units. Our increased support should go hand in hand with increased support from our Arab and European partners, including special forces who can contribute to the fight on the ground.

We should also work with the coalition and the neighbors to impose no-fly zones that will stop Assad from slaughtering civilians and the opposition from the air. Opposition forces on the ground with materiel support from the coalition could then help create safe areas where Syrians could remain in the country rather than fleeing toward Europe.

This combined approach would help enable the opposition to retake the remaining stretch of the Turkish border from ISIS, choking off its supply lines. It would also give us new leverage in the diplomatic process that Secretary Kerry is pursuing.

Of course, we've been down plenty of diplomatic dead ends before in this conflict, but we have models for how seemingly intractable multi-sectarian civil wars do eventually end. We can learn lessons from Lebanon and Bosnia about what it will take. And Russia and Iran have to face the fact that continuing to prop up a vicious dictator will not bring stability.

Right now I'm afraid President Putin is actually making things somewhat worse. Now, to be clear, though, there is an important role for Russian to help in resolving the conflict in Syria, and we have indicated a willingness to work with them toward an outcome that preserves Syria as a unitary nonsectarian state with protections for the rights of all Syrians, and to keep key state institutions intact. There is no alternative to a political transition that allows Syrians to end Assad's rule.

Now, much of this strategy on both sides of the border hinges on the roles of our Arab and Turkish partners, and we must get them to carry their share of the burden with military intelligence and financial contributions, as well as using their influence with fighters and tribes in Iraq and Syria. Countries like Jordan have offered more, and we should take them up on it, because ultimately our efforts will only succeed if the Arabs and Turks step up in a much bigger way. This is their fight and they need to act like it.

So far, however, Turkey has been more focused on the Kurds than on countering ISIS. And to be fair, Turkey has a long and painful history with Kurdish terrorist groups, but the threat from ISIS cannot wait. As difficult as it may be, we need to get Turkey to stop bombing Kurdish fighters in Syria who are battling ISIS and become a full partner in our coalition efforts against ISIS.

The United States should also work with our Arab partners to get them more invested in the fight against ISIS. At the moment they're focused in other areas because of their concerns in the region, especially the threat from Iran. That's why the Saudis, for example, shifted attention from Syria to Yemen. So we have to work out a common approach.

In September I laid out a comprehensive plan to counter Iranian influence across the region and its support for terrorist proxies such as Hezbollah and Hamas. We cannot view Iran and ISIS as separate challenges. Regional politics are too interwoven. Raising the confidence of our Arab partners and raising the costs to Iran for bad behavior will contribute to a more effective fight against ISIS.

And as we work out a broader regional approach, we should of course be closely consulting with Israel, our strongest ally in the Middle East. Israel increasingly shares with our Arabpartners and has the opportunity to do more in intelligence and joint efforts as well.

Now, we should have no illusions about how difficult the mission before us really is. We have to fit a lot of pieces together, bring along a lot of partners, move on multiple fronts at once. But if we press forward on both sides of the border, in the air and on the ground, as well as diplomatically, I do believe we can crush ISIS's enclave of terror.

And to support this campaign, Congress should swiftly pass an updated authorization to use military force. That will send a message to friend and foe alike that the United States is committed to this fight. The time for delay is over. We should get this done.

Now, the second element of our strategy looks beyond the immediate battlefield of Iraq and Syria to disrupt and dismantle global terrorist infrastructure on the ground and online. A terror pipeline that facilitates the flow of fighters, financing, arms, and propaganda around the world has allowed ISIS to strike at the heart of Paris last week, and an al-Qaida affiliate to do the same at Charlie Hebdo earlier this year.

ISIS is working hard to extend its reach, establish affiliates and cells far from its home base. And despite the significant setbacks it has encountered, not just with ISIS and its ambitious plans, but even al-Qaida, including the death of Osama bin Laden, they are still posing great threats to so many.

Let's take one example. We've had a lot of conversation about ISIS in the last week. Let's not forget al-Qaida. They still have the most sophisticated bomb makers, ambitious plotters, and active affiliates in places like Yemen and North Africa. So we can't just focus on Iraq and Syria. We need to intensify our counterterrorism efforts on a wider scope.

Most urgent is stopping the flow of foreign fighters to and from the war zones of the Middle East. Thousands, thousands, of young recruits have flocked to Syria from France, Germany, Belgium, the United Kingdom, and, yes, even the United States. Their western passports make it easier for them to cross borders and eventually return home, radicalized and battle-hardened.

Stemming this tide will require much better coordination and information-sharing among countries every step of the way. We should not stop pressing until Turkey, where most foreign fighters cross into Syria, finally locks down its border.

The United States and our allies need to know and share the identities of every fighter who has traveled to Syria. We also have to be smart and target interventions that will have the greatest impact. For example, we need a greater focus on shutting down key enablers who arrange transportation, documents, and more.

When it comes to terrorist financing, we have to go after the nodes that facilitate illicit trade and transactions. The U.N. Security Council should update its terrorism sanctions. They have a resolution that does try to block terrorist financing and other enabling activities. But we have to place more obligations on countries to police their own banks. And the United States, which has quite a record of success in this area, can share more intelligence to help other countries.

And, once and for all, the Saudis, the Qataris, and others need to stop their citizens from directly funding extremist organizations, as well as the schools and mosques around the world that have set too many young people on a path to radicalization.

When it comes to blocking terrorist recruitment, we have to identify the hot spots, the specific neighborhoods and villages, the prisons and schools, where recruitment happens in clusters, like the neighborhood in Brussels where the Paris attacks were planned. Through partnerships with local law enforcement and civil society, especially with Muslim community leaders, we have to work to tip the balance away from extremism in these hot spots.

Radicalization and recruitment also is happening online. There's no doubt we have to do a better job contesting online space, including websites and chat rooms, where jihadists communicate with followers. We must deny them virtual territory just as we deny them actual territory.

At the State Department, I built up a unit of communications specialists fluent in Urdu, Arabic, Somali, and other languages to battle with extremists online. We need more of that, including from the private sector. Social media companies can also do their part by swiftly shutting down terrorist accounts so they're not used to plan, provoke, or celebrate violence. Online or offline, the bottom line is that we are in a contest of ideas against an ideology of hate, and we have to win. Let's be clear, though. Islam is not our adversary. Muslims are peaceful and tolerant people and have nothing whatsoever to do with terrorism. The obsession in some quarters with a clash of civilization or repeating the specific words radical Islamic terrorism isn't just a distraction. It gives these criminals, these murderers, more standing than they deserve. It actually plays into their hands by alienating partners we need by our side.

Our priority should be how to fight the enemy. In the end, it didn't matter what kind of terrorist we called bin Laden. It mattered that we killed bin Laden. But we still can't close our eyes to the fact that there is a distorted and dangerous stream of extremism within the Muslim world that continues to spread. Its adherents are relatively few in number but capable of causing profound damage, most especially to their own communities, throughout an arc of instability that stretches from North and West Africa to Asia.

Overlapping conflicts, collapsing state structures, widespread corruption, poverty, and repression have created openings for extremists to exploit. Before the Arab spring, I warned that the region's foundations would sink into the sand without immediate reforms. Well, the need has only grown more urgent.

We have to join with our partners to do the patient, steady work of empowering moderates and marginalizing extremists, supporting democratic institutions and the rule of law, creating economic growth that supports stability, working to curb corruption, helping train effective and accountable law enforcement, intelligence, and counterterrorism services. As we do this, we must be building up a global counterterrorism infrastructure that is more effective and adaptable than the terror networks we're trying to defeat. When I became secretary of state, I was surprised to find that nearly a decade after 9/11 there was still no dedicated international vehicle to regularly convene key countries to deal with terrorist threats. So we created the Global Counterterrorism Forum, which now brings together nearly 30 countries, many from the Muslim world.

It should be a clearinghouse for directing assistance to countries that need it or mobilizing common action against threats. And let's not lose sight of the global cooperation needed to lock down loose nuclear material and chemical and biological weapons and keep them out of the hands of terrorists.

At the end of the day, we still must be prepared to go after terrorists wherever they plot, using all the tools at our disposal. That includes targeted strikes by U.S. military aircraft and drones, with proper safeguards, when there aren't any other viable options to deal with continuing imminent threats. All of this, stopping foreign fighters, blocking terrorist financing, doing battle in cyberspace, is vital to the war against ISIS, but it also lays the foundation for defusing and defeating the next threat and the one after that.

Now, the third element of our strategy has to be hardening our defenses at home and helping our partners do the same against both external and homegrown threats. After 9/11, the United States made a lot of progress breaking down bureaucratic barriers to allow for more and better information sharing among agencies responsible for keeping us safe. We still have work to do on this front, but by comparison Europe is way behind. Today, European nations don't even always alert each other when they turn away a suspected jihadist at the border, or when a passport is stolen. It seems like after most terrorist attacks we find out that the perpetrators were known to some security service or another, but too often the dots never get connected.

I appreciate how hard this is, especially given the sheer number of suspects and threats, but this has to change. The United States must work with Europe to dramatically and immediately improve intelligence sharing and counterterrorism coordination. European countries also should have the flexibility to enhance their border controls when circumstances warrant. And here at home, we face a number of our own challenges. The threat to airline security is evolving as terrorists develop new devices, like nonmetallic bombs. So our defenses have to stay at least one step ahead.

We know that intelligence gathered and shared by local law enforcement officers is absolutely critical to breaking up plots and preventing attacks. So they need all the resources and support we can give them. Law enforcement also needs the trust of residents and communities including, in our own country, Muslim Americans. Now, this should go without saying, but in the current climate it bears repeating. Muslim Americans are working every day on the front lines of the fight against radicalization.

Another challenge is how to strike the right balance of protecting privacy and security. Encryption of mobile communications presents a particularly tough problem. We should take the concerns of law enforcement and counterterrorism professionals seriously. They have warned that impenetrable encryption may prevent them from accessing terrorist communications and preventing a future attack. On the other hand, we know there are legitimate concerns about government intrusion, network security, and creating new vulnerabilities that bad actors can and would exploit. So we need Silicon Valley not to view government as its adversary. We need to challenge our best minds in the private sector to work with our best minds in the public sector to develop solutions that will both keep us safe and protect our privacy. Now is the time to solve this problem, not after the next attack.

Since Paris, no homeland security challenge is being more hotly debated than how to handle Syrian refugees seeking safety in the United States. Our highest priority, of course, must always be protecting the American people. So, yes, we do need to be vigilant in screening and vetting any refugees from Syria, guided by the best judgment of our security professionals in close coordination with our allies and partners. And Congress needs to make sure the necessary resources are provided for comprehensive background checks, drawing on the best intelligence we can get. And we should be taking a close look at the safeguards and the visa programs as well.

But we cannot allow terrorists to intimidate us into abandoning our values and our humanitarian obligations. Turning away orphans, applying a religious test, discriminating against Muslims, slamming the door on every Syrian refugee— that is just not who we are. We are better than that. And remember, many of these refugees are fleeing the same terrorists who threaten us. It would be a cruel irony indeed if ISIS can force families from their homes, and then also prevent them from ever finding new ones. We should be doing more to ease this humanitarian crisis, not less. We should lead the international community in organizing a donor conference and supporting countries like Jordan, who are sheltering the majority of refugees fleeing Syria.

And we can get this right. America's open, free, tolerant society is described by some as a vulnerability in the struggle against terrorism, but I actually believe it's one of our strengths. It reduces the appeal of radicalism and enhances the richness and resilience of our communities. This is not a time for scoring political points. When New York was attacked on 9/11 we had a Republican president, a Republican governor, and a Republican mayor. And I worked with all of them. We pulled together and put partisanship aside to rebuild our city and protect our country.

This is a time for American leadership. No other country can rally the world to defeat ISIS and win the generational struggle against radical jihadism. Only the United States can mobilize common action on a global scale. And that's exactly what we need. The entire world must be part of this fight, but we must lead it. There's been a lot of talk lately about coalitions. Everyone seems to want one. But there's not nearly as much talk about what it actually takes to make a coalition work in the heat and pressure of an international crisis. I know how hard this is because we've done it before.

To impose the toughest sanctions in history on Iran, to stop a dictator from slaughtering his people in Libya, to support a fledgling democracy in Afghanistan, we have to use every pillar of American power—military, and diplomacy; development, and economic, and cultural influence; technology, and, maybe most importantly, our values. That is smart power. We have to work with institutions and partners like NATO, the EU, the Arab League, and the U.N., strengthen our alliances and never get tired of old-fashioned, shoe-leather diplomacy. And if necessary, be prepared to act decisively on our own, just as we did to bring Osama bin Laden to justice. The United States and our allies must demonstrate that free people and free markets are still the hope of humanity.

This past week, as I watched the tragic scenes from France, I kept thinking back to a young man the world met in January, after the last attack in Paris. His name was Lassana, a Muslim immigrant from Mali, who worked at a kosher market. He said the market had become a new home and his colleagues and customers a second family. When the terrorists arrived and the gunfire began, Lassana risked his life to protect his Jewish customers. He moved quickly, hiding as many people as he could in the cold storage room, and then slipping out to help the police. I didn't know or care, he said, if they were Jews, or

Christians, or Muslims. We're all in the same boat. What a rebuke to the extremists' hatred.

The French government announced it would grant Lassana full citizenship. But when it mattered most, he proved he was a citizen already. That's the power of free people. That's what the jihadis will never understand and never defeat. And as we leave here today, let us resolved that we will go forward together. And we will do all we can to lead the world against this threat that threatens people everywhere."

Summary of Donald Trump proposal on national security and terrorism.

Trump supports increasing military spending, opposes the Iran nuclear arms deal, and believes that illegal immigration is a serious national security concern. Here is what he said,

"I just wanna say that we're gonna come out with some plans in a very short time. We're gonna be building up our military, we're gonna make our military so big and so strong and so great and it will be so powerful that I don't think we're ever going to have to use it. Nobody's gonna mess with us, that I can tell you, and we're going to have a president who's respected by Putin, who's respected by Iran, y'know?

Let's talk about, for two seconds, let's talk about the Iran deal. Now, Obama, Obama and his people call him the Supreme Leader, of Iran. Obama talks about the Supreme Leader. Well, I'm not calling him a supreme leader, but he said the other day that after this rip-off deal is completed he will never touch, do business with, the United States again. "We're finished with the United States." They're taking a hundred and fifty billion dollars, they're getting a deal that's gonna need - it's gonna go right into nuclear weapons, much sooner than you think. They're gonna self police, think of that one, they are going to go and self police. They got the twenty-four - they have twenty-four day provisions - and by the way, what people don't understand, the twenty-four day provision doesn't start, you know this right? It doesn't start for a long time before you get to it. The clock is ticking, it can take forever, we may never get in there. It is one of the dumbest deals and one of the weakest contracts I've ever seen of any kind. So, we are gonna do things in this country right! We're not gonna sign deals where we have four prisoners over there, and they're still there, and we don't even ask if one of them is there because he's a Christian. We have a writer, we have - the whole thing is absolutely insane. You know they asked the President, and they asked Secretary of State Kerry, who may be - you know I've been saying Hillary Clinton is the worst Secretary of State in the history of this country, right? Alright, I've been saying it, but it's possible - the world blew up around her, it blew up, the whole world is like a different place. It's possible that because of this deal, made by Secretary Kerry, who has absolutely no clue how to negotiate, it may be that he's going to supersede, and I understand that he may wanna run for President. He has no chance like she has no chance, so we're gonna see what happens.

We have many problems in our country, one of them is immigration. Now, I took a tremendous hit when I brought up illegal immigration when I announced I was running for president. And for two weeks I said - you know Rush Limbaugh, who's a great guy, he said - he has suffered more incoming, meaning the press, than anybody I have ever seen. So what happened is you have now found out what illegal immigration is all about, and I am so happy that I'm the one that brought it to the fore, because believe me it's a big problem. It is a big problem."

If we don't get tough, and we don't get smart — and fast — we're not going to have a country anymore -- there will be nothing left.

It's not just a national security issue. It is a quality of life issue.

If we want to protect the quality of life for all Americans — women and children, gay and straight, Jews and Christians and all people — then we need to tell the truth about Radical Islam.

Chapter five

Education.

The public educational system in the united states undoubtedly needs a lot of improvement. Stakeholders must identify the problems confronting public schools in the country. For instance, National Center for Education Statistics research says that roughly 19 percent of public school students are not able to finish high school. More than 70 percent are not qualified to enroll for a college degree. In short, public education seems to be declining compared to other developed nations. This deficiency in educational preparedness is something that the government has to realize right away. The self-esteem of teachers has been a perennial concern. Some of these professional tutors are underpaid or do not receive enough incentives that will serve as basis for motivation. Once this happens, efficient instructors are forced to seek employment elsewhere or look for other jobs that will guarantee higher compensation and more lucrative career options.

Politicians have long mentioned education in their speeches but the past two years it seemed to have happened more than ever. Many politicians seem to focus on how schools are failing, and their only solution is standardization, accountability and high stakes testing.

Summary of Hillary Clinton proposal on education

Hillary Clinton backed education reform, particularly the use of testing to improve standards. In 1992, when her husband was running for President, she received the now-famous "Letter to

Hillary Clinton," from Marc Tucker, the president of the National Center on Education and the Economy, which advocated a national curriculum, extensive testing, and an education system in which "most of the federal, state, district and union rules and regulations" that prevented big changes "are swept away."

Hillary Clinton also supported changing rules in order to make it easier for principals and school districts to get rid of problem teachers. In her 2000 Senate run, during a debate with her Republican opponent, Rick Lazio, she said, "I think we ought to streamline the due-process standards so that teachers that don't measure up would no longer be in the classroom." Some of Clinton's wealthy backers are still big supporters of the education-reform agenda, which the Obama Administration has also pursued aggressively. (Last year, it asked Congress for a fifty-per-cent increase in funding for charters.) But as Cooper pointed out during Sunday night's debate, Clinton has received the endorsement of two of the biggest teachers' unions, the American Federation of Teachers and the National Education Association, which are far less enthusiastic about charters and changes to work rules. On her campaign Web site, she pledges to "make high-quality education available to every child—in every zip code—in America," she said "Education should be the great door opener, and yet we know it often doesn't turn out that way. I think every child in this country deserves a good teacher in a good school, regardless of the ZIP code you live in." other things she promised to do in education sector includes

1. To launch a national campaign to modernize and elevate the profession of teaching. America is asking more of our educators than ever before. They are preparing our kids for a competitive economy, staying on top of new pedagogies, and filling gaps that we as a country have neglected—like giving low-income kids, English-language learners, and kids with disabilities the support they need to thrive. We ask so much of our educators, but we aren't setting them up for success. That's why Hillary will launch a national campaign to elevate and modernize the teaching profession, by preparing, supporting, and paying every child's teacher as if the future of our country is in their hands—because it is.

2. Provide every student in America an opportunity to learn computer science. There are more than half a million open jobs that require computing skills—across the country and in every major industry. But the majority of schools in the United States don't offer computer science. Hillary will provide states and school districts funding to help scale computer science instruction and lesson programs that improve student achievement or increase college enrollment and completion in CS Ed fields.

3. Rebuild America's schools. In cities and rural communities across America, there are public schools that are falling apart—schools where students are learning in classrooms with rodents and mold. That's unacceptable, and it has to change. That's why Hillary will build on the highly successful Build America Bonds program to provide cities and towns the capital they need to rebuild their schools. These "Modernize Every School Bonds" will double the Build America Bonds subsidy for

efforts to fix and modernize America's classrooms—from increasing energy efficiency and tackling asbestos to upgrading science labs and high-speed broadband.

4. Dismantle the school-to-prison pipeline. Schools should be safe places for students to learn and grow. But in too many communities, student discipline is overly harsh—and these harsh measures disproportionately affect African American students and those with the greatest economic, social, and academic needs. Hillary will work to dismantle the school-to-prison pipeline by providing $2 billion in support to schools to reform overly punitive disciplinary policies, calling on states to reform school disturbance laws, and encouraging states to use federal education funding to implement social and emotional support interventions.

Hillary has been working to improve and support our public schools for decades:

As a young law student working for Marian Wright Edelman, Hillary went undercover to investigate "segregation academies" in Alabama.

As first lady of Arkansas, she chaired the Arkansas Educational Standards Commission, fighting to raise academic standards, increase teacher salaries, and reduce class sizes.

As first lady of the United States, she chaired the first-ever convening on Hispanic children and youth, which focused on improving access to educational opportunities.

As a U.S. senator, she served on the Senate Health, Education and Labor Committee, as a key member shaping the No Child Left Behind Act, with the hope that it would bring needed resources and real accountability to improve educational opportunities for our most disadvantaged students.

Summary of Donald Trump proposal on education.

Here is what Donald Trump will do to the education sector if he is elected. Trump Would return education policy to the states and do away with Common Core education standards

Supports greatly reducing the size of the U.S. Department of Education

In a January 11, 2016 interview with The Wall Street Journal, Donald Trump said he would do "tremendous cutting" of the federal government. Education policy, he said, should be returned to the states, and he said he would end the Common Core education standards, which conservatives view as federal overreach. "Education should be local and locally managed," said Trump.

Asked about the Common Core during a radio interview with Hugh Hewitt in February 2015, Trump said, "I think that education should be local, absolutely. I think that for people in Washington to be setting curriculum and to be setting all sorts of standards for people living in Iowa and other places is ridiculous."

Trump said, in a speech at the South Carolina Tea Party Convention in January 2015, that the Department of Education could be "cut...way, way, way down."

In his 2000 book, The America We Deserve, Trump advocated for school choice, charter schools and vouchers. He argued that together they create a competitive system that improves education and offers an alternative to a public education model which "would set off every antitrust alarm bell at the Department of Justice and the Federal Trade Commission" if it were a traditional business.

Trump wants to Let schools compete: charters, vouchers, and magnets

Competition is why I'm very much in favor of school choice. Let schools compete for kids. I guarantee that if you forced schools to get better or close because parents didn't want to enroll their kids there, they would get better. Those schools that weren't good enough to attract students would close, and that's a good thing.

For two decades I've been urging politicians to open the schoolhouse doors and let parents decide which schools are best for their children. Professional educators look to claim that doing so would be the end of good public schools. Better charter or magnet schools would drain the top kids out of that system, or hurt the morale of those left behind. Suddenly, the excellence that comes from competition is being criticized.

Trump also believes that No federal government profit from student loans

A four-year degree today can be expensive enough to create six-figure debt. We can't forgive these loans, but we should take steps to help students.

The big problem is the federal government. There is no reason the federal government should profit from student loans. This only makes an already difficult problem worse. The Federal Student Loan Program turned a $41.3 billion profit in 2013.

These student loans are probably one of the only things that the government shouldn't make money from, and yet it does. And do you think this has anything to do with why schools continue to raise their tuition every year? Those loans should be viewed as an investment in America's future.

He really wants to Bring on the competition; tear down the union walls

Our public schools have grown up in a competition-free zone, surrounded by a very high union wall. Why aren't we shocked at the results? After all, teachers' unions are motivated by the same desires that move the rest of us. With more than 85% of their soft-money donations going to Democrats, teachers' unions know they can count on the politician they back to take a strong stand against school choice.

Our public schools are capable of providing a more competitive product than they do today. Look at some of the high school tests from earlier in this century and you'll wonder if they weren't college-level tests. And we've got to bring on the competition -open the schoolhouse doors and let parents choose the best school for their children.

Education reformers call this school choice, charter schools, vouchers, even opportunity scholarships. I call it competition-the American way.

Defenders of the status quo insist that parental choice means the end of public schools. Let's look at the facts. Right now, nine of ten children attend public schools. If you look at public education as a business- and with nearly $300 billion spent each year on K-through-twelve education, it's a very big business indeed-it would set off every antitrust alarm bell at the Department of Justice and the Federal Trade Commission. When teachers' unions say even the most minuscule program allowing school choice is a mortal threat, they're saying: If we aren't allowed to keep 90% of the market, we can't survive. When Bell Telephone had 90% of the market, a federal judge broke it up.

Who's better off? The kids who use vouchers to go to the school of their choice, or the ones who choose to stay in public school? All of them. That's the way it works in a competitive system.

Chapter six

Healthcare

While Americans feel the economy and jobs as well as foreign policy are bigger issues in this election year, there are varying opinions about how the next president of the United States should tackle healthcare, according to a Kaiser Family Foundation report.

The "Kaiser Health Tracking Poll: February 2016" shows 7 percent of democratic voters, 7 percent of republican voters and 10 percent of independent voters feel healthcare as the top issue in the 2016 election. But how would they like to see their next president handle healthcare?

The candidates have laid out healthcare plans running the gamut from Universal healthcare to single-payer systems to complete tear-down and rebuild. Here are key thoughts from the report.

1. Among all voters surveyed, 36 percent said lawmakers should build on the existing healthcare law to improve affordability and access. Democrats drove this group, with 54 percent saying they prefer to build on the existing healthcare law.

2. Thirty-four percent of the survey respondents feel universal coverage through a single government plan; 33 percent of Democrats are in favor of universal healthcare coverage.

3. Sixteen percent of the respondents want the current healthcare reform legislation repealed and not replaced; 13

percent want the legislation repealed and replaced with a Republican-sponsored alternative.

4. Sixty percent of Republicans want to repeal healthcare reform legislation whether it's replaced or not; however, 21 percent of Republicans would prefer to build on the existing law. Only 9 percent are in favor of universal healthcare through a government plan.

5. Among independents, 12 percent feel healthcare reform laws should be repealed and not replaced; 13 percent favor repealing and replacing in favor of a Republican-sponsored alternative. Thirty-six percent want to build on the existing law and 9 percent are in favor of universal coverage through a single government plan.

Summary of Hillary Clinton proposal on healthcare

"As your president, I want to build on the progress we've made. I'll do more to bring down health care costs for families, ease burdens on small businesses, and make sure consumers have the choices they deserve. And frankly, it is finally time for us to deal with the skyrocketing out-of-pocket health costs, and particularly runaway prescription drug prices."

Hillary Clinton has led and will continue to lead the fight to expand health care access for every American—even when it means standing up to special interests. When insurance companies spent millions to stop her efforts to reform health care in the '90s, she refused to give up. Instead, she worked across the aisle to help pass the Children's Health Insurance Program. Today, it covers 8 million kids. She has never given up on the fight for universal coverage.

Her plans on healthcare includes

1. Defend and expand the Affordable Care Act, which covers 20 million people. Hillary will stand up to Republican-led attacks on this landmark law—and build on its success to bring the promise of affordable health care to more people and make a "public option" possible. She will also support letting people over 55 years old buy into Medicare.

2. Bring down out-of-pocket costs like copays and deductibles. American families are being squeezed by rising out-of-pocket health care costs. Hillary believes that workers should share in slower growth of national health care spending through lower costs.

3. Reduce the cost of prescription drugs. Prescription drug spending accelerated from 2.5 percent in 2013 to 12.6 percent in 2014. It's no wonder that almost three-quarters of Americans believe prescription drug costs are unreasonable. Hillary believes we need to demand lower drug costs for hardworking families and seniors. Read more here.

4. Fight for health insurance for the lowest-income Americans in every state by incentivizing states to expand Medicaid—and make enrollment through Medicaid and the Affordable Care Act easier.

5. Expand access to affordable health care to families regardless of immigration status. Hillary will expand access to affordable health care to families regardless of immigration status by allowing families to buy health insurance on the health exchanges regardless of their immigration status.

6. Expand access to rural Americans, who often have difficulty finding quality, affordable health care. Hillary will explore cost-effective ways to make more health care providers eligible for telehealth reimbursement under Medicare and other programs, including federally qualified health centers and rural health clinics.

7. Defend access to reproductive health care. Hillary will work to ensure that all women have access to preventive care, affordable contraception, and safe and legal abortion.

8. Double funding for community health centers, and support the healthcare workforce: As part of her comprehensive health care agenda, Hillary is committed to doubling the funding for primary-care services at community health centers over the next decade. Hillary also supports President Obama's call for a near tripling of the size of the National Health Service Corp.

Summary of Donald Trump proposal on healthcare

Donald Trump Has a healthcare reform plan based on "free market principles"

And Would repeal Obamacare, reduce barriers to the interstate sale of health insurance, institute a full tax deduction for insurance premium payments for individuals, make Health Saving Accounts inheritable, require price transparency, block-grant Medicaid to the states, and allow for more overseas drug providers through lowered regulatory barriers

On March 2, 2016, Trump released a seven-point plan for healthcare reform, which he described as based on "free market principles." He stated that he would repeal

Obamacare, reduce barriers to the interstate sale of health insurance, institute a full tax deduction for insurance premium payments for individuals, make Health Saving Accounts inheritable, require price transparency, block-grant Medicaid to the states, and allow for more overseas drug providers through lowered regulatory barriers. Trump added that enforcing immigration laws could reduce healthcare costs.

At the eighth Republican presidential primary debate on February 6, 2016, Donald Trump discussed his position on healthcare, and whether it is closer to Hillary Clinton's or Bernie Sanders': "I think I'm closer to common sense. We are going to repeal Obamacare. ... We are going to replace Obamacare with something so much better. And there are so many examples of it. And I will tell you, part of the reason we have some people laughing, because you have insurance people that take care of everybody up here. I am self-funded. The only one they're not taking care of is me. We have our lines around each state. The insurance companies are getting rich on Obamacare. The insurance companies are getting rich on health care and health services and everything having to do with health. We are going to end that. We're going to take out the artificial boundaries, the artificial lines. We're going to get a plan where people compete, free enterprise. They compete. So much better. In addition to that, you have the health care savings plans, which are excellent. What I do say is, there will be a certain number of people that will be on the street dying and as a Republican, I don't want that to happen. We're going to take care of people that are dying on the street because there will be a group of people that are not going to be able to even think in terms of private or anything else and we're going to take care of those people. And I think everybody on this stage would have to agree, you're not going to let people die, sitting in the middle of a street in any city in this country."

Trump suggested that he supported universal healthcare on September 27, 2015. "I am going to take care of everybody. I don't care if it costs me votes or not. Everybody's going to be taken care of much better than they're taken care of now," he said.

In a July 2015 Forbes interview on how Trump would replace Obamacare, a Trump spokesperson said, "Mr. Trump will be proposing a health plan that will return authority to the states and operate under free market principles. Mr. Trump's plan will provide choice to the buyer, provide individual tax relief for health insurance and keep plans portable and affordable. The plan will break the health insurance company monopolies and allow individuals to buy across state lines."

Trump spoke at the Iowa Freedom Summit in January 2015 where he said, "Someone has to repeal and replace Obamacare." Explaining his position, Trump said, "[Obamacare is] a total catastrophe. It kicks in in 2016 and it will be a disaster. People are closing shops. Doctors are quitting the business. I have a friend who was a doctor and he says he has more accountants than patients. He needs that because it is complicated and terrible."

In September 2013, Trump called Obamacare "a total disaster" and stated it "will shut down this country."

As an alternative to Obamacare, Trump recommended in 2011 allowing people to "purchase health-care plans across state lines" because "[c]ompetition makes everything better and more affordable."

In his 2000 book, The America We Deserve, Trump wrote, "We must have universal health care." He suggested that this initiative be modeled after the Federal Employees Health Benefits Program, saying, "Our objective [should be] to make reforms for the moment and, longer term, to find an equivalent of the single-payer plan that is affordable, well-administered, and provides freedom of choice. Possible? The good news is, yes. There is already a system in place-the Federal Employees Health Benefits Program-that can act as a guide for all healthcare reform. It operates through a centralized agency that offers considerable range of choice. While this is a government program, it is also very much market-based."

Chapter seven

Taxation

WalletHub surveyed over 1,000 Americans last year as regards to taxation, and the results offer some interesting insights into the psyche of the typical taxpayer: When asked which they considered to be most important, "tax equality," "tax fairness" or "whatever is best for the economy," respondents overwhelmingly placed the economy at the end of the priority queue. More than 60 percent said tax fairness was the most important of the three issues, while nearly 20 percent sided with tax equality, and only 18 percent put economic prosperity above all else.

This likely would not have been the case a few years ago during the depths of the Great Recession. In addition to reflecting popular sentiment about a system that many feel only works for an elite few, the fact that we have the luxury to feel this way could be construed as economically encouraging. One of the biggest areas of agreement among taxpayers, regardless of age or party affiliation, concerns how complicated the tax code has become. Eighty percent of survey respondents consider it to be "complex" or "too complex," while only 2 percent report it being "simple" or "very simple." What's more, 44 percent of people think the fairest possible tax code would have fewer deductions than we do now, while only about 31 percent think more deductions are in order.

This seems to reflect the long-held belief that tax code complexity enables those with the most means to exploit loopholes that may not be apparent to the general population.

Summary of Hillary Clinton proposal on taxation

Hillary Clinton believes that we need an economy that works for everyone, not just those at the top. But when it comes to taxes, too often the wealthiest and the largest corporations are playing by a different set of rules than hardworking families.

Hillary is committed to restoring basic fairness in our tax code and ensuring that the wealthiest Americans and large corporations pay their fair share, while providing tax relief to working families. That's not only fair, it's good for economic growth, because she will use the proceeds to create good-paying jobs here in America—and make bold investments that leave our economy more competitive over the long run.

As president, Hillary will:

Restore basic fairness to our tax code. Hillary will implement a "fair share surcharge" on multi-millionaires and billionaires and fight for measures like the Buffett Rule to ensure the wealthiest Americans do not pay a lower tax rate than hardworking middle-class families. She'll close loopholes that create a private tax system for the most fortunate, and she'll ensure multi-million-dollar estates are paying their fair share of taxes.

Close corporate and Wall Street tax loopholes and invest in America. Hillary will close tax loopholes like inversions that reward companies for shifting profits and jobs overseas. She will charge an "exit tax" for companies leaving the U.S. to settle up on their untaxed foreign earnings. She will close tax loopholes that let Wall Street money managers pay lower rates than some middle-class families. And she'll reward businesses that invest in good-paying jobs here in the United States.

Simplify and cut taxes for small businesses so they can hire and grow. The smallest businesses, with one to five employees, spend 150 hours and $1,100 per employee on federal tax compliance. That's more than 20 times higher than the average for far larger firms. We've got to fix that.

Provide tax relief to working families from the rising costs they face. For too many years, middle-class families have been squeezed by rising costs for everything from child care to health care to affording college. Hillary will offer relief from these rising costs, including tax relief for Americans facing excessive out-of-pocket health care costs and for those caring for an ill or elderly family member.

Pay for ambitious investments in a fiscally responsible way. Hillary believes that we can afford to pay for ambitious, progressive investments in good-paying jobs, debt-free college, and other measures to strengthen growth, broaden opportunity, and reduce inequality. Hillary will use the proceeds from ensuring the wealthiest and the largest corporations pay their fair share to pay for these investments without adding to the debt.

Summary of Donald Trump proposal on taxation

Too few Americans are working, too many jobs have been shipped overseas, and too many middle class families cannot make ends meet. This tax plan directly meets these challenges with four simple goals:

Tax relief for middle class Americans: In order to achieve the American dream, let people keep more money in their pockets and increase after-tax wages.

Simplify the tax code to reduce the headaches Americans face in preparing their taxes and let everyone keep more of their money.

Grow the American economy by discouraging corporate inversions, adding a huge number of new jobs, and making America globally competitive again.

Doesn't add to our debt and deficit, which are already too large.

The Trump Tax Plan Achieves These Goals

If you are single and earn less than $25,000, or married and jointly earn less than $50,000, you will not owe any income tax. That removes nearly 75 million households – over 50% – from the income tax rolls. They get a new one page form to send the IRS saying, "I win," those who would otherwise owe income taxes will save an average of nearly $1,000 each.

All other Americans will get a simpler tax code with four brackets – 0%, 10%, 20% and 25% – instead of the current seven. This new tax code eliminates the marriage penalty and the Alternative Minimum Tax (AMT) while providing the lowest tax rate since before World War II.

No business of any size, from a Fortune 500 to a mom and pop shop to a freelancer living job to job, will pay more than 15% of their business income in taxes. This lower rate makes corporate inversions unnecessary by making America's tax rate one of the best in the world.

No family will have to pay the death tax. You earned and saved that money for your family, not the government. You paid taxes on it when you earned it.

The Trump Tax Plan Is Revenue Neutral

The Trump tax cuts are fully paid for by:

Reducing or eliminating most deductions and loopholes available to the very rich.

A one-time deemed repatriation of corporate cash held overseas at a significantly discounted 10% tax rate, followed by an end to the deferral of taxes on corporate income earned abroad.

Reducing or eliminating corporate loopholes that cater to special interests, as well as deductions made unnecessary or redundant by the new lower tax rate on corporations and business income. We will also phase in a reasonable cap on the deductibility of business interest expenses.

Too many companies – from great American brands to innovative startups – are leaving America, either directly or through corporate inversions. The Democrats want to outlaw inversions, but that will never work. Companies leaving is not the disease, it is the symptom. Politicians in Washington have let America fall from the best corporate tax rate in the industrialized world in the 1980's (thanks to Ronald Reagan) to the worst rate in the industrialized world. That is unacceptable. Under the Trump plan, America will compete with the world and win by cutting the corporate tax rate to 15%, taking our rate from one of the worst to one of the best.

This lower tax rate cannot be for big business alone; it needs to help the small businesses that are the true engine of our economy. Right now, freelancers, sole proprietors, unincorporated small businesses and pass-through entities are taxed at the high personal income tax rates. This treatment stifles small businesses. It also stifles tax reform because efforts to reduce loopholes and deductions available to the very rich and special interests end up hitting small businesses and job creators as well. The Trump plan addresses this challenge head on with a new business income tax rate within the personal income tax code that matches the 15% corporate tax rate to help these businesses, entrepreneurs and freelancers grow and prosper.

These lower rates will provide a tremendous stimulus for the economy – significant GDP growth, a huge number of new jobs and an increase in after-tax wages for workers.

The Trump Tax Plan Ends The Unfair Death Tax

The death tax punishes families for achieving the American dream. Therefore, the Trump plan eliminates the death tax. The Trump Tax Plan Is Fiscally Responsible The Trump tax cuts are fully paid for by:

Reducing or eliminating deductions and loopholes available to the very rich, starting by steepening the curve of the Personal Exemption Phaseout and the Pease Limitation on itemized deductions. The Trump plan also phases out the tax exemption on life insurance interest for high-income earners, ends the current tax treatment of carried interest for speculative partnerships that do not grow businesses or create jobs and are not risking their own capital, and reduces or eliminates other loopholes for the very rich and special interests. These reductions and eliminations will not harm the economy or hurt the middle class. Because the Trump plan introduces a new business income rate within the personal income tax code, they will not harm small businesses either.

A one-time deemed repatriation of corporate cash held overseas at a significantly discounted 10% tax rate. Since we are making America's corporate tax rate globally competitive, it is only fair that corporations help make that move fiscally responsible. U.S.-owned corporations have as much as $2.5 trillion in cash sitting overseas. Some companies have been leaving cash overseas as a tax maneuver. Under this plan, they can bring their cash home and put it to work in America while benefitting from the newly-lowered corporate tax rate that is globally competitive and no longer requires parking cash overseas. Other companies have cash overseas for specific business units or activities. They can leave that cash overseas, but they will still have to pay the one-time repatriation fee.

An end to the deferral of taxes on corporate income earned abroad. Corporations will no longer be allowed to defer taxes on income earned abroad, but the foreign tax credit will remain in place because no company should face double taxation.

Reducing or eliminating some corporate loopholes that cater to special interests, as well as deductions made unnecessary or redundant by the new lower tax rate on corporations and business income. We will also phase in a reasonable cap on the deductibility of business interest expenses.

Chapter eight

Immigration

America has always welcomed immigrants who choose to enter the country the legal way. Every year immigration lawyers help thousands of clients begin a new life in the country while work permits and other types of visas are granted to individuals and families by federal immigration officials.

However, illegal immigration continues to be a major problem with as many as 11 million individuals and families currently living illegally in the country.

It is no secret that there are numerous problems that the United States faces due to illegal immigration and illegal immigrants. This is why there are immigration and border laws to protect its citizens. However, the influx of people entering from across the border continues to be a major hindrance and with the Obama administration's skewed immigration policies in support of illegal immigration instead of protecting Americans, the problem gets even deeper.

Americans remain unsafe and insecure

One of the biggest problems that harm Americans is lost jobs and lower wages. With over 11 million illegal aliens in the country, millions of American citizens find it difficult to find a job or are out of work.

In addition, an increase in the number of crimes and domestic terrorism poses a serious threat. The two most recent, gruesome killings of innocent Americans, Kathryn Steinle and Marlyn Pharis, are evidence of the burgeoning threat to the country's citizens. These were two hard working, innocent citizens whose lives were snuffed out by illegal immigrants with criminal records who still roamed the streets of America freely.

They chose not to work with an immigration attorney and do it the right way. One of these dedicated legal professionals can be found right here: USAttorneys.com.

A waste of taxpayer dollars

Illegal immigration has caused a number of Americans to lose their jobs and home due to foreclosure. Even some of the lesser desirable jobs have been usurped by illegal immigrants who are willing to work at wages that are impossible for Americans to even try to make ends meet. To add salt to the wound, estimates by Americans for Legal Immigration (ALIPAC) are that American taxpayer resources worth over $125 billion are stolen by illegal immigrants. Most importantly, it is taxpayer dollars that are used to fund education, healthcare, infrastructure, and meet court and prison costs of illegal immigrants. Food stamps and welfare that can be used to benefit Americans are now being used by illegal immigrants.

The politics of illegal immigration

For the most part, there is a long list of lawmakers and activists in many states who are politically responsible for the chaos, death, and destruction by illegal immigration and amnesty programs. While not every illegal immigrant can be tagged a criminal beyond the fact that they entered the country illegally and are possibly involved in document fraud, too many go on to commit worse crimes that are often hushed up.

According to immigration lawyers, a major percentage of crimes by illegal aliens could be prevented if the existing immigration laws were enforced and sanctuary cities changed their ways and became a thing of the past.

Every year, potentially thousands of Americans are exposed to crimes by illegal immigrants who are saved by sanctuary cities that ignore requests from federal immigration agencies such as ICE to detain illegal immigrants in prison until they are cleared for deportation. With Republicans successful so far in putting a halt to the Obama administration's immigration reforms policy, one can only hope it will reduce the problems and keep Americans safer.

Summary of Hillary Clinton proposal on immigration

Hillary has been committed to the immigrant rights community throughout her career. As president, she will work to to fix our broken immigration system and stay true to our fundamental American values: that we are a nation of immigrants, and we treat those who come to our country with dignity and respect—and that we embrace immigrants, not denigrate them.

Hillary Clinton will do the following to the immigration system as the president.

Introduce comprehensive immigration reform. Hillary will introduce comprehensive immigration reform with a pathway to full and equal citizenship within her first 100 days in office. It will treat every person with dignity, fix the family visa backlog, uphold the rule of law, protect our borders and national security, and bring millions of hardworking people into the formal economy.

End the three- and 10-year bars. The three- and 10-year bars force families—especially those whose members have different citizenship or immigration statuses—into a heartbreaking dilemma: remain in the shadows, or pursue a green card by leaving the country and loved ones behind.

Defend President Obama's executive actions—known as DACA and DAPA—against partisan attacks. The Supreme Court's deadlocked decision on DAPA was a heartbreaking reminder of how high the stakes are in this election. Hillary believes DAPA is squarely within the president's authority and won't stop fighting until we see it through. The estimated 5 million people eligible for DAPA—including DREAMers and parents of Americans and lawful residents—should be protected under the executive actions.

Do everything possible under the law to protect families. If Congress keeps failing to act on comprehensive immigration reform, Hillary will enact a simple system for those with sympathetic cases—such as parents of DREAMers, those with a history of service and contribution to their communities, or those who experience extreme labor violations—to make their case and be eligible for deferred action.

Enforce immigration laws humanely. Immigration enforcement must be humane, targeted, and effective. Hillary will focus resources on detaining and deporting those individuals who pose a violent threat to public safety, and ensure refugees who seek asylum in the U.S. have a fair chance to tell their stories.

End family detention and close private immigration detention centers. Hillary will end family detention for parents and children who arrive at our border in desperate situations and close private immigrant detention centers.

Expand access to affordable health care to all families. We should let families—regardless of immigration status—buy into the Affordable Care Act exchanges. Families who want to purchase health insurance should be able to do so.

Promote naturalization. Hillary will work to expand fee waivers to alleviate naturalization costs, increase access to language programs to encourage English proficiency, and increase outreach and education to help more people navigate the process.

Summary of Donald Trump proposal on immigration

The three core principles of Donald J. Trump's immigration plan

When politicians talk about "immigration reform" they mean: amnesty, cheap labor and open borders. The Schumer-Rubio immigration bill was nothing more than a giveaway to the corporate patrons who run both parties.

Real immigration reform puts the needs of working people first – not wealthy globetrotting donors. We are the only country in the world whose immigration system puts the needs of other nations ahead of our own. That must change. Here are the three core principles of real immigration reform:

1. A nation without borders is not a nation. There must be a wall across the southern border.

2. A nation without laws is not a nation. Laws passed in accordance with our Constitutional system of government must be enforced.

3. A nation that does not serve its own citizens is not a nation. Any immigration plan must improve jobs, wages and security for all Americans

Trump is gojng to make Mexico Pay For The Wall

For many years, Mexico's leaders have been taking advantage of the United States by using illegal immigration to export the crime and poverty in their own country (as well as in other Latin American countries). They have even published pamphlets on how to illegally immigrate to the United States. The costs for the United States have been extraordinary: U.S. taxpayers have been asked to pick up hundreds of billions in healthcare costs, housing costs, education costs, welfare costs, etc. Indeed, the annual cost of free tax credits alone paid to illegal immigrants quadrupled to $4.2 billion in 2011. The effects on jobseekers have also been disastrous, and black Americans have been particularly harmed.

The impact in terms of crime has been tragic. In recent weeks, the headlines have been covered with cases of criminals who crossed our border illegally only to go on to commit horrific crimes against Americans. Most recently, an illegal immigrant from Mexico, with a long arrest record, is charged with breaking into a 64 year-old woman's home, crushing her skull and eye sockets with a hammer, raping her, and murdering her. The Police Chief in Santa Maria says the "blood trail" leads straight to Washington.

In 2011, the Government Accountability Office found that there were a shocking 3 million arrests attached to the incarcerated alien population, including tens of thousands of violent beatings, rapes and murders.

Meanwhile, Mexico continues to make billions on not only our bad trade deals but also relies heavily on the billions of dollars in remittances sent from illegal immigrants in the United States back to Mexico ($22 billion in 2013 alone).

In short, the Mexican government has taken the United States to the cleaners. They are responsible for this problem, and they must help pay to clean it up.

The cost of building a permanent border wall pales mightily in comparison to what American taxpayers spend every single year on dealing with the fallout of illegal immigration on their communities, schools and unemployment offices.

Mexico must pay for the wall and, until they do, the United States will, among other things: impound all remittance payments derived from illegal wages; increase fees on all temporary visas issued to Mexican CEOs and diplomats (and if necessary cancel them); increase fees on all border crossing cards – of which we issue about 1 million to Mexican nationals each year (a major source of visa overstays); increase fees on all NAFTA worker visas from Mexico (another major source of overstays); and increase fees at ports of entry to the United States from Mexico [Tariffs and foreign aid cuts are also options]. We will not be taken advantage of anymore.

Defend The Laws And Constitution Of The United States

America will only be great as long as America remains a nation of laws that lives according to the Constitution. No one is above the law. The following steps will return to the American people the safety of their laws, which politicians have stolen from them:

Triple the number of ICE officers. As the President of the ICE Officers' Council explained in Congressional testimony: "Only approximately 5,000 officers and agents within ICE perform the lion's share of ICE's immigration mission...Compare that to the Los Angeles Police Department at approximately 10,000 officers. Approximately 5,000 officers in ICE cover 50 states, Puerto Rico and Guam, and are attempting to enforce immigration law against 11 million illegal aliens already in the interior of the United States. Since 9-11, the U.S. Border Patrol has tripled in size, while ICE's immigration enforcement arm, Enforcement and Removal Operations (ERO), has remained at relatively the same size." This will be funded by accepting the recommendation of the Inspector General for Tax Administration and eliminating tax credit payments to illegal immigrants.

Nationwide e-verify. This simple measure will protect jobs for unemployed Americans.

Mandatory return of all criminal aliens. The Obama Administration has released 76,000 aliens from its custody with criminal convictions since 2013 alone. All criminal aliens must be returned to their home countries, a process which can be aided by canceling any visas to foreign countries which will not accept their own criminals, and making it a separate and additional crime to commit an offense while here illegally.

Detention—not catch-and-release. Illegal aliens apprehended crossing the border must be detained until they are sent home, no more catch-and-release.

Defund sanctuary cities. Cut-off federal grants to any city which refuses to cooperate with federal law enforcement.

Enhanced penalties for overstaying a visa. Millions of people come to the United States on temporary visas but refuse to leave, without consequence. This is a threat to national security. Individuals who refuse to leave at the time their visa expires should be subject to criminal penalties; this will also help give local jurisdictions the power to hold visa overstays until federal authorities arrive. Completion of a visa tracking system – required by law but blocked by lobbyists – will be necessary as well.

Cooperate with local gang task forces. ICE officers should accompany local police departments conducting raids of violent street gangs like MS-13 and the 18th street gang, which have terrorized the country. All illegal aliens in gangs should be apprehended and deported. Again, quoting Chris Crane: "ICE Officers and Agents are forced to apply the Deferred Action for Childhood Arrivals (DACA) Directive, not to children in schools, but to adult inmates in jails. If an illegal-alien inmate simply claims eligibility, ICE is forced to release the alien back into the community. This includes serious criminals who have committed felonies, who have assaulted officers, and who prey on children...ICE officers should be required to place detainers on every illegal alien they encounter in jails and prisons, since these aliens not only violated immigration laws, but then went on to engage in activities that led to their arrest by police; ICE officers should be required to issue Notices to Appear to all illegal aliens with criminal convictions, DUI convictions, or a gang affiliation; ICE should be working with any state or local drug or gang task force that asks for such assistance

End birthright citizenship. This remains the biggest magnet for illegal immigration. By a 2:1 margin, voters say it's the wrong policy, including Harry Reid who said "no sane country" would give automatic citizenship to the children of illegal immigrants.

Put American Workers First

Decades of disastrous trade deals and immigration policies have destroyed our middle class. Today, nearly 40% of black teenagers are unemployed. Nearly 30% of Hispanic teenagers are unemployed. For black Americans without high school diplomas, the bottom has fallen out: more than 70% were employed in 1960, compared to less than 40% in 2000. Across the economy, the percentage of adults in the labor force has collapsed to a level not experienced in generations. As CBS news wrote in a piece entitled "America's incredible shrinking middle class": "If the middle-class is the economic backbone of America, then the country is developing osteoporosis."

The influx of foreign workers holds down salaries, keeps unemployment high, and makes it difficult for poor and working class Americans – including immigrants themselves and their children – to earn a middle class wage. Nearly half of all immigrants and their US-born children currently live in or near poverty, including more than 60 percent of Hispanic immigrants. Every year, we voluntarily admit another 2 million new immigrants, guest workers, refugees, and dependents, growing our existing all-time historic record population of 42 million immigrants. We need to control the admission of new low-earning workers in order to: help wages grow, get teenagers back to work, aid minorities' rise into the middle class, help schools and communities falling behind, and to ensure our immigrant members of the national family become part of the American dream.

Additionally, we need to stop giving legal immigrant visas to people bent on causing us harm. From the 9/11 hijackers, to the Boston Bombers, and many others, our immigration system is being used to attack us. The President of the immigration caseworkers union declared in a statement on ISIS: "We've become the visa clearinghouse for the world."

Here are some additional specific policy proposals for long-term reform:

Increase prevailing wage for H-1Bs. We graduate two times more Americans with STEM degrees each year than find STEM jobs, yet as much as two-thirds of entry-level hiring for IT jobs is accomplished through the H-1B program. More than half of H-1B visas are issued for the program's lowest allowable wage level, and more than eighty percent for its bottom two. Raising the prevailing wage paid to H-1Bs will force companies to give these coveted entry-level jobs to the existing domestic pool of unemployed native and immigrant workers in the U.S., instead of flying in cheaper workers from overseas. This will improve the number of black, Hispanic and female workers in Silicon Valley who have been passed over in favor of the H-1B program. Mark Zuckerberg's personal Senator, Marco Rubio, has a bill to triple H-1Bs that would decimate women and minorities.

Requirement to hire American workers first. Too many visas, like the H-1B, have no such requirement. In the year 2015, with 92 million Americans outside the workforce and incomes collapsing, we need companies to hire from the domestic pool of unemployed. Petitions for workers should be mailed to the unemployment office, not USCIS.

End welfare abuse. Applicants for entry to the United States should be required to certify that they can pay for their own housing, healthcare and other needs before coming to the U.S.

Jobs program for inner city youth. The J-1 visa jobs program for foreign youth will be terminated and replaced with a resume bank for inner city youth provided to all corporate subscribers to the J-1 visa program.

Refugee program for American children. Increase standards for the admission of refugees and asylum-seekers to crack down on abuses. Use the monies saved on expensive refugee programs to help place American children without parents in safer homes and communities, and to improve community safety in high crime neighborhoods in the United States.

Immigration moderation. Before any new green cards are issued to foreign workers abroad, there will be a pause where employers will have to hire from the domestic pool of unemployed immigrant and native workers. This will help reverse women's plummeting workplace participation rate, grow wages, and allow record immigration levels to subside to more moderate historical averages.

Chapter nine

Gun policy.

The fatal shooting of 49 people at a Florida nightclub on June 12, 2016 is the latest in a long series of mass killings to restoke the national debate over gun ownership, with the Senate doing battle over the issue during the week after the tragedy.

The gunman in Orlando, Omar Mateen, was armed with a handgun and an assault rifle; in addition to those he killed, he wounded another 53, and he himself was killed by police.

The horrific attack — the biggest mass shooting in U.S. history — came less than six months after two suspects opened fire in a California social services center, killing 14 and injuring 21.

Despite the outpouring of grief and sympathy that followed the San Bernardino incident, though, the very next day the Senate rejected a bill to tighten background check requirements on would-be gun buyers — just as it did in 2013, shortly after a lone gunman killed 27 at Sandy Hook Elementary School in Newtown, Conn., including 20 children, six adults and himself.

Whether 2016 will be any different remains to be seen. In fact, the issue of how to strike a balance between gun rights and public safety has been a political hot potato for years, and one that Congress has dealt with gingerly — too gingerly, in the view of groups favoring tighter firearms regulations. But both candidates have promised to do something about this issue.

Summary of Hillary Clinton proposal on gun policy.

Too many families in America have suffered—and continue to suffer—from gun violence. It's the leading cause of death among young African American men—more than the following nine causes combined. America cannot go on like this. As president, Hillary will:

Expand background checks to more gun sales—including by closing the gun show and internet sales loopholes—and strengthen the background check system by getting rid of the so-called "Charleston Loophole."

Take on the gun lobby by removing the industry's sweeping legal protection for illegal and irresponsible actions (which makes it almost impossible for people to hold them accountable), and revoking licenses from dealers who break the law.

Keep guns out of the hands of domestic abusers, other violent criminals, and the severely mentally ill by supporting laws that stop domestic abusers from buying and owning guns, making it a federal crime for someone to intentionally buy a gun for a person prohibited from owning one, and closing the loopholes that allow people suffering from severe mental illness to purchase and own guns. She will also support work to keep military-style weapons off our streets.

Hillary has a record of advocating for commonsense approaches to reduce gun violence:

As first lady, she co-convened a White House Summit on School Violence after the Columbine tragedy, and strongly defended the Brady Bill, which instituted federal background checks on some gun sales.

As senator, she co-sponsored and voted for legislation that would close the gun show loophole, voted against the dangerous immunity protections for gun dealers and manufacturers, and co-sponsored legislation to extend and reinstate the assault weapons ban.

As a candidate, she is honored to have the endorsement of many groups working to take on the epidemic of violence, including the Brady Campaign to Prevent Gun Violence, the Newtown Action Alliance, and Everytown for Gun Safety— including Moms Demand Action for Gun Sense in America.

Summary of Donald Trump proposal on gun policy

Here is what Donald Trump opinion on gun control,

The Second Amendment to our Constitution is clear. The right of the people to keep and bear Arms shall not be infringed upon. Period.

The Second Amendment guarantees a fundamental right that belongs to all law-abiding Americans. The Constitution doesn't create that right – it ensures that the government can't take it away. Our Founding Fathers knew, and our Supreme Court has upheld, that the Second Amendment's purpose is to guarantee our right to defend ourselves and our families. This is about self-defence, plain and simple.

It's been said that the Second Amendment is America's first freedom. That's because the Right to Keep and Bear Arms protects all our other rights. We are the only country in the world that has a Second Amendment. Protecting that freedom is imperative. Here's how we will do that:

Enforce The Laws On The Books

We need to get serious about prosecuting violent criminals. The Obama administration's record on that is abysmal. Violent crime in cities like Baltimore, Chicago and many others is out of control. Drug dealers and gang members are given a slap on the wrist and turned loose on the street. This needs to stop.

Several years ago there was a tremendous program in Richmond, Virginia called Project Exile. It said that if a violent felon uses a gun to commit a crime, you will be prosecuted in federal court and go to prison for five years – no parole or early release. Obama's former Attorney General, Eric Holder, called that a "cookie cutter" program. That's ridiculous. I call that program a success. Murders committed with guns in Richmond decreased by over 60% when Project Exile was in place – in the first two years of the program alone, 350 armed felons were taken off the street.

Why does that matter to law-abiding gun owners? Because they're the ones who anti-gun politicians and the media blame when criminals misuse guns. We need to bring back and expand programs like Project Exile and get gang members and drug dealers off the street. When we do, crime will go down and our cities and communities will be safer places to live.

Here's another important way to fight crime – empower law-abiding gun owners to defend themselves. Law enforcement is great, they do a tremendous job, but they can't be everywhere all of the time. Our personal protection is ultimately up to us.

That's why I'm a gun owner, that's why I have a concealed carry permit, and that's why tens of millions of Americans have concealed carry permits as well. It's just common sense. To make America great again, we're going to go after criminals and put the law back on the side of the law-abiding.

Fix Our Broken Mental Health System

Let's be clear about this. Our mental health system is broken. It needs to be fixed. Too many politicians have ignored this problem for too long.

All of the tragic mass murders that occurred in the past several years have something in common – there were red flags that were ignored. We can't allow that to continue. We need to expand treatment programs, because most people with mental health problems aren't violent, they just need help. But for those who are violent, a danger to themselves or others, we need to get them off the street before they can terrorize our communities. This is just common sense.

And why does this matter to law-abiding gun owners? Once again, because they get blamed by anti-gun politicians, gun control groups and the media for the acts of deranged madmen. When one of these tragedies occurs, we can count on two things: one, that opponents of gun rights will immediately exploit it to push their political agenda; and two, that none of their so-called "solutions" would have prevented the tragedy in the first place. They've even admitted it.

We need real solutions to address real problems. Not grandstanding or political agendas.

Defend The Rights of Law-Abiding Gun Owners

GUN AND MAGAZINE BANS. Gun and magazine bans are a total failure. That's been proven every time it's been tried. Opponents of gun rights try to come up with scary sounding phrases like "assault weapons", "military-style weapons" and "high capacity magazines" to confuse people. What they're really talking about are popular semi-automatic rifles and standard magazines that are owned by tens of millions of Americans. Law-abiding people should be allowed to own the firearm of their choice. The government has no business dictating what types of firearms good, honest people are allowed to own.

BACKGROUND CHECKS. There has been a national background check system in place since 1998. Every time a person buys a gun from a federally licensed gun dealer – which is the overwhelming majority of all gun purchases – they go through a federal background check. Study after study has shown that very few criminals are stupid enough to try and pass a background check – they get their guns from friends/family members or by stealing them. So the overwhelming majority of people who go through background checks are law-abiding gun owners. When the system was created, gun owners were promised that it would be instant, accurate and fair. Unfortunately, that isn't the case today. Too many states are failing to put criminal and mental health records into the system – and it should go without saying that a system's only going to be as effective as the records that are put into it. What we need to do is fix the system we have and make it work as intended. What we don't need to do is expand a broken system.

NATIONAL RIGHT TO CARRY. The right of self-defense doesn't stop at the end of your driveway. That's why I have a concealed carry permit and why tens of millions of Americans do too. That permit should be valid in all 50 states. A driver's license works in every state, so it's common sense that a concealed carry permit should work in every state. If we can do that for driving – which is a privilege, not a right – then surely we can do that for concealed carry, which is a right, not a privilege.

MILITARY BASES AND RECRUITING CENTERS.

Banning our military from carrying firearms on bases and at recruiting centers is ridiculous. We train our military how to safely and responsibly use firearms, but our current policies leave them defenseless. To make America great again, we need a strong military. To have a strong military, we need to allow them to defend themselves.

Chapter ten

Climate change

As Bernie Sanders so simply said in the debate, "Terrorism can't bring down our civilization, but climate change can." the New York times has identified climate change as the biggest challenge of 2016. "At the end of 2015, we asked what you felt was the greatest challenge facing the United States in the coming year. Over a thousand readers responded, and while their answers varied widely, a few common themes emerged. Climate change.

The climate crisis dwarfs all other issues. Climate change has put weather on steroids. The oceans are becoming acidified. The adverse consequences are already having a disparate impact on the poor. And it will only get worse. We need to use less energy, replace fossil fuels with renewable energy (like wind and solar) for our remaining energy needs, and adopt land use practices that stop deforestation and unsustainable agriculture. Even if we stopped all carbon pollution today, impacts would continue to increase for some time due to the time lag in our climate system. It is important that we both move to eliminate fossil fuels, and begin to prepare for the impacts we can't avoid through smarter planning and actions to improve the resilience of communities to stronger and more frequent storms, droughts, heat waves and sea level rise.

Below are the presidential front runners proposal to tackling climate change if elected.

Summary of Hillary Clinton proposal on climate change

"I won't let anyone take us backward, deny our economy the benefits of harnessing a clean energy future, or force our children to endure the catastrophe that would result from unchecked climate change." (Hillary Clinton Nov 2015)

Hillary Clinton plans to

1. Generate enough renewable energy to power every home in America, with half a billion solar panels installed by the end of Hillary's first term.

2. Cut energy waste in American homes, schools, hospitals and offices by a third and make American manufacturing the cleanest and most efficient in the world.

3. Reduce American oil consumption by a third through cleaner fuels and more efficient cars, boilers, ships, and trucks.

Hillary's plan will deliver on the pledge President Obama made at the Paris climate conference—without relying on climate deniers in Congress to pass new legislation. She will reduce greenhouse gas emissions by up to 30 percent in 2025 relative to 2005 levels and put the country on a path to cut emissions more than 80 percent by 2050.

Hillary will:

Defend, implement, and extend smart pollution and efficiency standards, including the Clean Power Plan and standards for cars, trucks, and appliances that are already helping clean our air, save families money, and fight climate change.

Launch a $60 billion Clean Energy Challenge to partner with states, cities, and rural communities to cut carbon pollution and expand clean energy, including for low-income families. Read the fact sheet here.

Invest in clean energy infrastructure, innovation, manufacturing and workforce development to make the U.S. economy more competitive and create good-paying jobs and careers. Read the fact sheet here.

Ensure safe and responsible energy production. As we transition to a clean energy economy, we must ensure that the fossil fuel production taking place today is safe and responsible and that areas too sensitive for energy production are taken off the table. Read the fact sheet here.

Reform leasing and expand clean energy production on public lands and waters tenfold within a decade.

Cut the billions of wasteful tax subsidies oil and gas companies have enjoyed for too long and invest in clean energy.

Cut methane emissions across the economy and put in place strong standards for reducing leaks from both new and existing sources.

Revitalize coal communities by supporting locally driven priorities and make them an engine of U.S. economic growth in the 21st century, as they have been for generations. Read the fact sheet here.

Make environmental justice and climate justice central priorities by setting bold national goals to eliminate lead poisoning within five years, clean up the more than 450,000 toxic brownfield sites across the country, expand solar and energy efficiency solutions in low-income communities, and create an Environmental and Climate Justice Task Force. Read the fact sheet here.

Promote conservation and collaborative stewardship. Hillary will keep public lands public, strengthen protections for our natural and cultural resources, increase access to parks and public lands for all Americans, as well as harness the immense economic potential they offer through expanded renewable energy production, a high quality of life, and a thriving outdoor economy. Read the fact sheet here.

Summary of Donald Trump proposal on climate change.

Donald Trump says he is "not a big believer in global warming." He has called it "a total hoax," "bullshit" and "pseudoscience."

Donald Trump would be the only national leader in the world to dismiss the science of climate change should he become president, putting him out of step even with Syrian president Bashar al-Assad, Zimbabwe's Robert Mugabe and Kim Jong-un, the leader of North Korea.

The potential isolation of the US on climate change has been laid bare by a new Sierra Club report which found universal acceptance of climate science among the leaders of the 195 countries recognized by the US state department.

Close US allies such as Britain, Israel, Canada and France all have heads of government who have voiced their understanding that the world is warming primarily due to human activities. Even totalitarian or undemocratic leaders accept mainstream climate science, with Assad calling for nations to "respond more effectively" to the issue and Kim supporting a tree-planting initiative to mitigate greenhouse gases. The Zimbabwean president, Robert Mugabe, has labelled climate change a "major global challenge".

By contrast, Trump, the Republican presidential nominee, has called global warming "bullshit" and a "hoax" that was "created by and for the Chinese in order to make US manufacturing noncompetitive". Trump has vowed to remove the US from the Paris climate accord, which was agreed by 195 countries last year in an attempt to curb planet-warming carbon dioxide emissions. He has also threatened to dismantle the Environmental Protection Agency, which has come under sustained fire from Republicans over its role in Barack Obama's emissions-cutting Clean Power Plan. Trump appears to be speaking for a small but notable minority, with Yale finding that 10% of Americans are "dismissive" of climate change as an issue.

Chapter eleven

Wall Street and bank regulation and reform

The financial crisis showed how irresponsible behavior in the financial sector can devastate the lives of everyday Americans—costing 9 million workers their jobs, driving 5 million families out of their homes, and wiping out more than $13 trillion in household wealth.

One result of the 2008 financial crisis was a big Democratic victory in elections that November, giving the party control of the White House and both houses of Congress. That empowered the party to shape the post crisis regulatory regime, through Dodd-Frank. In the 2016 campaign, Democrats and Republicans are fighting over the impact and future of the law. Here are their proposals on wallstreet regulation and reform.

Summary of Hillary Clinton proposal on wall street/bank regulation and reform.

Hillary Clinton has long stood up to Wall Street – going back to her time as New York Senator, when she warned against abuses nearly a year before the crisis hit. She has a plan to reduce the risk of future crises and make our financial system fairer and more accountable. She said "Our banking system is still too complex and too risky. ... While institutions have paid large fines and in some cases admitted guilt, too often it has seemed that the human beings responsible get off with limited consequences—or none at all, even when they've already pocketed the gains. This is wrong, and on my watch, it will change."

Hillary's plan will tackle dangerous risks in the financial system:

Impose a risk fee on the largest financial institutions. Big banks and financial companies would be required to pay a fee based on their size and their risk of contributing to another crisis.

Close loopholes that let banks make risky investments with taxpayer money. The Volcker Rule prohibits banks from making risky trading bets with taxpayer-backed money—one of the core protections of the post-financial crisis Wall Street reforms. However, under current law these banks can still invest billions through hedge funds, which are exempt from this rule. Hillary would close that loophole and strengthen the law.

Hold senior bankers accountable when a large bank suffers major losses. When a large bank suffers major losses with sweeping consequences, senior managers should lose some or all of their bonus compensation.

Make sure no financial firm is ever too big or too risky to be managed effectively. Hillary's plan would give regulators more authority to force overly complex or risky firms—including banks, hedge funds and other non-bank financial institutions—to reorganize, downsize, or break apart.

Tackle financial dangers of the "shadow banking" system. Hillary's plan will enhance transparency and reduce volatility in the "shadow banking system," which includes certain activities of hedge funds, investment banks, and other non-bank financial companies.

Impose a tax on high-frequency trading. The growth of high-frequency trading has unnecessarily placed stress on our markets, created instability, and enabled unfair and abusive trading strategies. Hillary would impose a tax on harmful high-frequency trading and reform rules to make our stock markets fairer, more open, and transparent.

Hillary would also hold both corporations and individuals on Wall Street accountable by:

Prosecuting individuals when they break the law. Hillary would extend the statute of limitations for prosecuting major financial frauds, enhance whistleblower rewards, and provide the Department of Justice and the Securities and Exchange Commission with more resources to prosecute wrongdoing.

Holding executives accountable when they are responsible for their subordinates' misconduct. Hillary believes that when corporations pay large fines to the government for violating the law, those fines should cut into the bonuses of the executives who were responsible for or should have caught the problem. And when egregious misconduct happens on an executive's watch, that executive should lose his or her job.

Holding corporations accountable when they break the law. Hillary will make sure that corporations can't treat penalties for breaking the law as merely a cost of doing business, so we can put an end to the patterns of corporate wrongdoing that we see too often today.

Summary of Donald Trump proposal on wallstreet/banks regulation and reform.

Republican presidential candidate Donald Trump said he will release an economic plan in two weeks that will undo nearly all of the financial reforms that went into effect in 2010. He also said he would take power away from the Federal Reserve and allow Congress to audit its decision making

He has suggested buying back government debt at a discount if interest rates go up

He would repeal the Dodd-Frank Act, enacted in 2010 to promote U.S. financial stability by improving accountability and increasing transparency in the financial system, protecting consumers, ending "too big to fail," and eliminating bailout.

Trump said his comments in a CNBC interview on May 6, 2016, about defaulting on debt were mischaracterized. "I said if we can buy back government debt at a discount, in other words, if interest rates go up and we can buy bonds back at a discount – if we are liquid enough as a country, we should do that. In other words, we can buy back debt at a discount," Trump said. He added that the U.S. will never have to default on debt "because you print the money."

During an interview with Fortune on April 19, 2016, Donald Trump praised Federal Reserve Chairwoman Janet Yellen, but said he supports "proposals that would take power away from the Fed, and allow Congress to audit the U.S. central bank's decision making." When asked about Yellen, Trump said, "I think she's [Janet Yellen] done a serviceable job. I don't want to comment on reappointment, but I would be more inclined to put other people in." Trump also commented on low-interest rates, saying, "The best thing we have going for us is that interest rates are so low. There are lots of good things that could be done that aren't being done, amazingly. ... People think the Fed should be raising interest rates. If rates are 3% or 4% or whatever, you start adding that kind of number to an already reasonably crippled economy in terms of what we produce, that number is a very scary number."

In October 2015, Trump said the Dodd-Frank Act was "terrible" and that he would "absolutely" repeal the law. "Under Dodd-Frank, the regulators are running the banks. The bankers are petrified of the regulators. And the problem is that the banks aren't loaning money to people who will create jobs," Trump said.

In an interview with Bloomberg's Mark Halperin in August 2015, Trump said he appreciated the low interest rates set by the Federal Reserve as a businessman, but expressed concern for the "bubble" they could create. "I like low interest rates. From the country's standpoint, I'm just not sure it's a very good thing, because I really do believe we're creating a bubble." When asked if he approved of the Volcker Rule, Trump said, "Well I'm not sure if [Paul Volcker] likes it, but if he's — you know what, honestly, Mark, if he's happy, I'm happy. He was a terrific guy. I've met him a few times. And I thought he was terrific. But I think his policy and his demeanor — there was something very solid about him. His demeanor were [sic] very good."

In April 2009, Trump said he partially supported how the Obama administration was handling financial institutions in jeopardy. He said, "I'm not saying I agree with everything [Obama's] doing. I do agree with what they're doing with the banks. Whether they fund them or nationalize them, it doesn't matter, but you have to keep the banks going. Beyond that, I'm not so sure I agree with it, because I...I am worried, ultimately, about inflation. If you take this much money and keep pouring it into the economy, I worry about what's going to happen in two years with respect to not only interest rates, but inflation."

Chapter twelve

Foreign trade

Foreign trade of the United States comprises the international imports and exports of the United States, one of the world's most significant economic markets. The country is among the top three global importers and exporters. The country has trade relations with many other countries. Within that, the trade with Europe and Asia is predominant. To fulfill the demands of the industrial sector, the country has to import mineral oil and iron ore on a large scale. Machinery, cotton yarn, toys, mineral oil, lubricants, steel, tea, sugar, coffee, and many more items are traded. The country's export list includes food grains like wheat, corn, and soybean. Aeroplane, cars, computers, paper, and machine tools required for different industries. United States trade policy has varied widely through various American historical and industrial periods. As a major developed nation, the U.S. has relied heavily on the import of raw materials and the export of finished goods. Because of the significance for American economy and industry, much weight has been placed on trade policy by elected officials and business leaders. Despite their differences on international trade, the 2016 presidential candidates find agreement on one issue: the Trans-Pacific Partnership. Hillary Clinton and Donald Trump oppose the trade deal because they believe it will cause Americans to lose jobs.

Summary of Hillary Clinton proposal on foreign trade.

Hillary Clinton will,

1.Supports the reauthorization of the Export-Import Bank

2. Opposes the Trans-Pacific Partnership; instead supports trade agreements that would raise wages, increase prosperity, create more new, good jobs for Americans, and protect our security.

On October 28, 2015, Hillary Clinton called the reauthorization of the Export-Import Bank a "no-brainer." She added, "For the life of me, I don't understand the arguments [against it]. The Export-Import Bank's sole purpose is to support United States business abroad.

On July 26, 2016, Virginia Gov. Terry McAuliffe (D) said that Clinton would support the Trans-Pacific Partnership (TPP) trade deal as president if the agreement were revised in some ways. He said, "I worry that if we don't do TPP, at some point China's going to break the rules -- but Hillary understands this. Once the election's over, and we sit down on trade, people understand a couple things we want to fix on it but going forward we got to build a global economy." When asked if he thought Clinton would support TPP, McAuliffe said, "Yes. Listen, she was in support of it. There were specific things in it she wants fixed."

McAuliffe's spokesman issued the following statement clarifying what the governor told Politico: "While Governor McAuliffe is a supporter of the TPP, he has no expectation Secretary Clinton would change her position on the legislation and she has never told him anything to that effect."

Clinton campaign chairman John Podesta weighed in on McAuliffe's statement, writing in a tweet, "Love Gov. McAuliffe, but he got this one flat wrong. Hillary opposes TPP BEFORE and AFTER the election. Period. Full stop."

On July 25, 2016, Gene Sperling, "a top economic adviser to the Clinton campaign," said that "Hillary Clinton is going to put new trade initiatives, including the maligned Trans-Pacific Partnership, in the rear-view mirror if elected and instead focus on 'things that are clear job creators...like infrastructure, immigration reform, higher education relief, family medical leave,'" according to Politico. Sperling continued, "What she [Clinton] has said is she is against it [the Trans-Pacific Partnership] now, she is against in the lame duck and she's against it afterwards, and I do believe that when she starts her administration, she is going to want to be focused on unifying Democrats."

On May 5, 2016, Clinton said that "she would oppose a vote on the Trans-Pacific Partnership trade accord during a lame-duck session of Congress," according to The Washington Post. Clinton said, "I oppose the TPP agreement — and that means before and after the election."

During a campaign rally in Youngstown, Ohio, on March 12, 2016, Hillary Clinton criticized the auto provisions of the Trans-Pacific Partnership (TPP) trade deal. She said, "We can not let rules of origin allow China — or anyone else, but principally China — to go around trade agreements. It's one of the reasons why I oppose the Trans-Pacific Partnership because when I saw what was in it, it was clear to me there were too many loopholes, too many opportunities for folks to be taken advantage of."

During the first Democratic debate, on October 13, 2015, Clinton defended her decision to oppose the Trans-Pacific Partnership (TPP) trade deal after supporting the pact while she was secretary of state. Clinton said, "You know, take the trade deal. I did say, when I was secretary of state, three years ago, that I hoped it would be the gold standard. It was just finally negotiated last week, and in looking at it, it didn't meet my standards. My standards for more new, good jobs for Americans, for raising wages for Americans. And I want to make sure that I can look into the eyes of any middle-class American and say, 'this will help raise your wages.' And I concluded I could not."

On October 7, 2015, Clinton said she does not support the Trans-Pacific Partnership (TPP) trade deal, putting her at odds with President Barack Obama and his administration. In an interview with PBS Newshour, she said she was concerned that the deal would not do enough to create jobs, raise wages for Americans, and advance national security. "As of today, I am not in favor of what I have learned about it," Clinton said. She added, "I don't believe it's going to meet the high bar I have set."

In a June 2015 interview with Jon Ralston of Ralston Reports, Clinton was asked if she would vote for trade promotion authority if she were still in the Senate. Clinton answered, "At this point, probably not because it's a process vote and I don't want to say it's the same as TPP. Right now I'm focused on making sure we get trade adjustment assistance and I certainly would not vote for it unless I were absolutely confident we would get trade adjustment assistance."

On June 15, 2015, CNN outlined 45 times when Clinton expressed her support for the Trans-Pacific Partnership (TPP) trade deal.

During an April 2015 speech, Clinton said, "Any trade deal has to produce jobs and raise wages and increase prosperity and protect our security," but she did not specifically address whether or not she supported President Barack Obama's Trans-Pacific Partnership (TPP) trade deal, a departure from her previous comments in support of the deal.

In November 2012, during a speech at Techport Australia, Clinton praised the TPP. She said, "This TPP sets the gold standard in trade agreements to open free, transparent, fair trade, the kind of environment that has the rule of law and a level playing field. And when negotiated, this agreement will cover 40 percent of the world's total trade and build in strong protections for workers and the environment."

Summary of Donald Trump proposal on foreign trade.

Donald Trump,

Advocates for fair trade and has called NAFTA "a disaster"

Describes trade promotion authority and the Trans-Pacific Partnership as "bad, bad deal[s] for American businesses, for workers, for taxpayers"

Has proposed steep tariffs on imported goods

During a Meet the Press interview on July 24, 2016, Trump discussed trade, saying that he will "impose tariffs — in the range of 15 percent to 35 percent — on companies like Indiana-based Carrier, which is moving its operations to Mexico," according to The Hill. Trump said, "If they're going to fire all their people, move their plant to Mexico, build air conditioners, and think they're going to sell those air conditioners to the United States, there's going to be a tax." Todd then said that "the import-tariff plan wouldn't pass muster at the WTO." Trump replied, "Then we're going to renegotiate or we're going to pull out. These trade deals are a disaster. You know, the World Trade Organization is a disaster."

In a speech delivered on June 28, 2016, Donald Trump explained how he would change America's "failed trade policy" by rejecting the Trans-Pacific Partnership trade deal, appointing the best trade negotiators, renegotiating and potentially withdrawing from the North American Free Trade Agreement (NAFTA), and labeling China a currency manipulator. In his prepared speech, titled "Declaring American Economic Independence," Trump warned his supporters that "Hillary Clinton, and her campaign of fear, will try to spread the lie that these actions will start a trade war. She has it completely backwards. Hillary Clinton unleashed a trade war against the American worker when she supported one terrible trade deal after another – from NAFTA to China to South Korea. A Trump Administration will end that war by getting a fair deal for the American people. The era of economic surrender will finally be over. A new era of prosperity will finally begin. America will be independent once more."

Donald Trump said on February 18, 2016, that he would send cease and desist letters to China, Mexico and other U.S. trade partners for "ripping us off." He added, "And when I say cease-and-desist orders, maybe it'd be equivalent. Maybe I'll do it with my mouth."

Trump advocated for fair trade and called NAFTA "a disaster" on September 27, 2015. "We will either renegotiate it or we will break it because you know every agreement has an end," said Trump.

In a statement released to The Daily Caller in May 2015, Trump criticized the Trans-Pacific Partnership, saying, "Yet again, the politicians are allowing our president to reinforce the lack of respect countries like China and Japan now have for the United States. They will devalue their currency, exploit our trade agreements, continue to destroy our economy and put Americans out of work. Politicians are all talk and no action. Instead of fast tracking TPP, Congress should pass legislation that holds China and Japan accountable for currency manipulation. This would send a message to the world that there are consequences for cheating the United States."

EPILOGUE

A lot of promises have been made by the two presidential candidate front runners, but having been highlighted as regards to their background and their proposals on how to tackle some of the pressing need facing America today a big question is left to be answered, hence

HILLARY CLINTON AND DONALD TRUMP WHO SUITS THE WHITE HOUSE?

www.ingramcontent.com/pod-product-compliance
Lightning Source LLC
Chambersburg PA
CBHW052002280526
45793CB00005B/816